WONDER PMO

A guide to set-up the PMO

DHANANJAY GOKHALE

notionpress.com

INDIA · SINGAPORE · MALAYSIA

Notion Press

Old No. 38, New No. 6
McNichols Road, Chetpet
Chennai - 600 031

First Published by Notion Press 2019
Copyright © Dhananjay Gokhale 2019
All Rights Reserved.

ISBN 978-1-64587-821-6

This book has been published with all efforts taken to make the material error-free after the consent of the author. However, the author and the publisher do not assume and hereby disclaim any liability to any party for any loss, damage, or disruption caused by errors or omissions, whether such errors or omissions result from negligence, accident, or any other cause.

While every effort has been made to avoid any mistake or omission, this publication is being sold on the condition and understanding that neither the author nor the publishers or printers would be liable in any manner to any person by reason of any mistake or omission in this publication or for any action taken or omitted to be taken or advice rendered or accepted on the basis of this work. For any defect in printing or binding the publishers will be liable only to replace the defective copy by another copy of this work then available.

Contents

Preface 7
Acknowledgements 11

Chapter 01   PM & PMO Oath 13
Chapter 02   What is PMO? 23
Chapter 03   P(2)M(L)O 29
Chapter 04   The Basics of PM 37
Chapter 05   PM and PMO 49
Chapter 06   The Name-Sake PMO 55
Chapter 07   4 Baskets of Contributory PMO 67
Chapter 08   Functions of the Contributory PMO 77
Chapter 09   Competency Assessment & Development! 93
Chapter 10   PM Competency Assessment 101

                10.1   The Objective of the Project Manager 103
                10.2   Context of PM Competency 106
                10.3   Need of PM Competency Assessment 108
                10.4   Project Management – a 3D Model! 109
                10.5   7 Verbs and 9 Nouns of Project
                        Management 111
                10.6   What is Competency? 114

10.7	Constituents of PM Competency	116
10.8	Grades of Project Management Competency	118
10.9	Background of the Case	122
10.10	Why Interview? Why Not Any Other Method?	123
10.11	What-If	124
10.12	Interviews – Interesting & Intriguing	126
10.13	Tough Behaviors	128
10.14	Use of My Experiences in Psychological Types	132
10.15	In Communications…	133
10.16	Parameters Defined for Assessments	137
10.17	Covering the Parameters in the Interview	138
10.18	Data and Related Inferences	140
10.19	Who Can Help Improving These Areas?	143
10.20	The Results	144
10.21	Detailed Quantitative Analysis	145
10.22	SkillWillFit Matrix	148
10.23	Stakeholders Involved & Their Roles	149
10.24	Pathways to Solutions	150
10.25	Role of PMO	152
10.26	PMO Handling Attitudinal Issues at Grade 4	160

Chapter 11   The Position & Potential Issues 171

Chapter 12   The Contributory PMO 181

Chapter 13   Set the Ball Rolling 187

Chapter 14   Conclusion 199

References for Answers *201*

DGtal Products *204*

Our Training & Consulting Services *206*

Preface

The organization should NOT have a PMO!

Got surprised with this lead-line? But that should be the aspiration of a contributory PMO. Every person in the organization should work as a contributory PMO and hence there would not be a need to have a separate entity called PMO.

"How can we make the business more adaptive, responsive and thus more profitable in a rapidly changing multi-project environment?"

The contributory PMO asks and answers the above question. And hence the aspiration is that every individual in the organization should ask and answer this. This is the state where there is no need to have separate entity of PMO.

Till then one must setup, and sustainably run the contributory PMO.

The project & program management office (PMO) is a key to ensure that project management is effectively applied across the organization. The sound principle of democracy, moulded a bit – "For, By and Of the Project Managers!" is the key for the success of the PMO.

There should be a home for these roaming buffalos of project & program management!

This book **"PMO: A wonderland – What Works & What Doesn't?"** takes you along to practically appreciate the contribution of PMO. This book also throws a light on hurdles involved and suggests solutions in setting up & sustainably running the PMO in successful manner.

The online course on **PMO: A wonderland – What Works & What Doesn't?** is available.

Watch trailer https://vimeo.com/ondemand/pmowonderland

Do watch the glimpses on https://vimeo.com/dgtal/pmosample

I have written it based on my numerous assignments on PMO setup in last 17 years. This is one of the best offering that I have! **It is a must watch & read by everyone in the field of project management.** It elaborates...

- ✓ **63 strings** of PM.
- ✓ **12 characteristics** of namesake & contributory PMO.
- ✓ **11 functions** of contributory PMO.
- ✓ **50 parameters** of PM competency assessment & development.
- ✓ **9 issues** that one needs to tackle while setting up a PMO.
- ✓ **8 effective actions** to set up the PMO.

Learning Objectives:

During and at the end of this learning intervention, the participants shall be able to.

- Appreciate the expression of 'wonder' in the context of PMO.
- List 7 verbs and 9 nouns used in eth project & program management.

- Draw the model of connect amongst project, program, organization and the PMO.
- Identify the causes of the issues they are facing related to project & program management.
- List and elaborate the characteristics of 'name-sake' PMO.
- Spot the existence of the characteristics of the 'name-sake' PMO in their organization.
- List the 4 baskets of the PMO Support.
- List at least 7 functions of the Contributory PMO in all the 4 baskets of the PMO Support.
- Describe the Project & Program Management concept with examples.
- List the 5 grades of the project & program management competency assessment with the example of the exhibition of grade characteristics.
- Appreciate the important role of the PMO in assessing & developing the PM competency.
- Assess the PM competencies with the help of external expert.
- List the 4 issues involved in the PM competency development.
- Suggest the solutions for combinations of the above issues.
- Tackle the potential issues in setting up the contributory PMO.
- Reduce or as a best case avoid any of the issues back at their work in PMO.
- List and elaborate the characteristics of 'contributory' PMO.
- Set the contributory PMO with the help of external expert.

- Develop the career path for self and colleagues in the context of PMO.

- Develop their competencies in becoming a professional project & program management service provider.

Welcome!

To the **Wonderland of PMO.**

Acknowledgements

No work can be done alone by any individual. There are many known – unknown people constantly help directly or indirectly. So is the case with this book as well. Writing and publishing a book is a huge task. I must express my gratitude to all those knowns & unknowns! I must express heartfelt thanks to all those who directly and indirectly contributed to this book. Here are some known who contributed directly.

Dr. Mrudula Samak, PMP®

Swati Kadu, PMP®

Nivedita Kulkarni, PMP®, PMI-ACP®, SAFe® Agilist

Kartiki Patil

Basu Iyer

Notion Press Team

Dr Mrudula drafted the workbook, assessments in the books. Those form a very foundational aspect of the book. In fact the very first draft was a transcription of my speeches. And Mrudula started contributing her work on this book right since then! Swati did the review of the book while adding to the assessments. The complete book was checked by Nivedita. Kartiki and Basu are the people who developed the illustrations. And of course, Notion Press team, did a systematic job of publishing. Without Shaunak's support the videos and its platform was simply not possible.

Although this book **"Wonderland of PMO"** is an expression of my learnings in last two decades, I must thank all the organizations who allowed me and gave the opportunity to assist them in taking the project & program management & leadership competency to sustainable contributory level.

Regards,

– Dhananjay Gokhale

Chapter 01

PM & PMO Oath

The **project & program management office (PMO)** is a key to ensure that project & program management is effectively applied across the organization. The sound principle of democracy, reads as **"For, By and Of the people"** molded a bit as – **"For, By and Of the Project & Program Managers!"** is the key for the **success of the PMO.**

To give a metaphor, like buffalos that roam on the grass-field, project & program management is found at specific spots within an organization, as well as on alterative grazing grounds depending on the season and the time. So, there should be a home for these roaming buffalos of project & program management!

Of late, PMO is becoming a watchword in the industry. It is indeed a good sign. However, one needs to follow certain discipline to seek the maximum yield.

The book takes you along to practically appreciate the contribution of PMO. The book also throws a light on hurdles involved in setting up and sustainably running the PMO in successful manner.

I sincerely welcome you to the "Wonderland of PMO – What Works & What Doesn't?" The book focuses on many important areas. They are...

1. PMO as a Wonder.
2. 63 strings of project & program management.
3. Fundamental connection between project & program management with PMO.
4. One real life example of a senior leader demanding the PMO set-up for the name-sake.
5. Characteristics of the name-sake PMO.
6. 4 baskets of the PMO support.
7. Functions of PMO.
8. Competency Development! – the most important role of the PMO.
9. Deep-dive in PM Competency Assessment & Development with the help of my book.

10. The organizational position & issues in setting the PMO.

11. Characteristics of the Contributory PMO.

12. Actions and tips for setting up the contributory PMO.

We will be elaborating these topics as we move along. There shall be small quizzes that you would have to solve at the end of each chapter.

PM Oath & PMO Oath!

Before we move forward on this journey, let's understand the guiding principles. It is like a lighthouse to a ship. The PM Oath and the PMO Oath will explain the guiding principle. I crafted the PM Oath in the year 2007. Many project & program managers approach me regularly stating the use of this oath.

The most common feedback is "The PM Oath reduces the frustration. At time we forgot the basic value addition and we get unwarrantedly attached to PM. We start hating the changes, ambiguities, chaos in and around the project. That is the time the PM Oath and the PMO Oath helps."

The PMO Oath is crafted in late 2017. At times people working in PMO come under the social pressures. They get afraid of loss & lack of formal power, thanklessness of the job. It is the time the PMO Oath comes handy and reminds the context of PMO.

The PM Oath

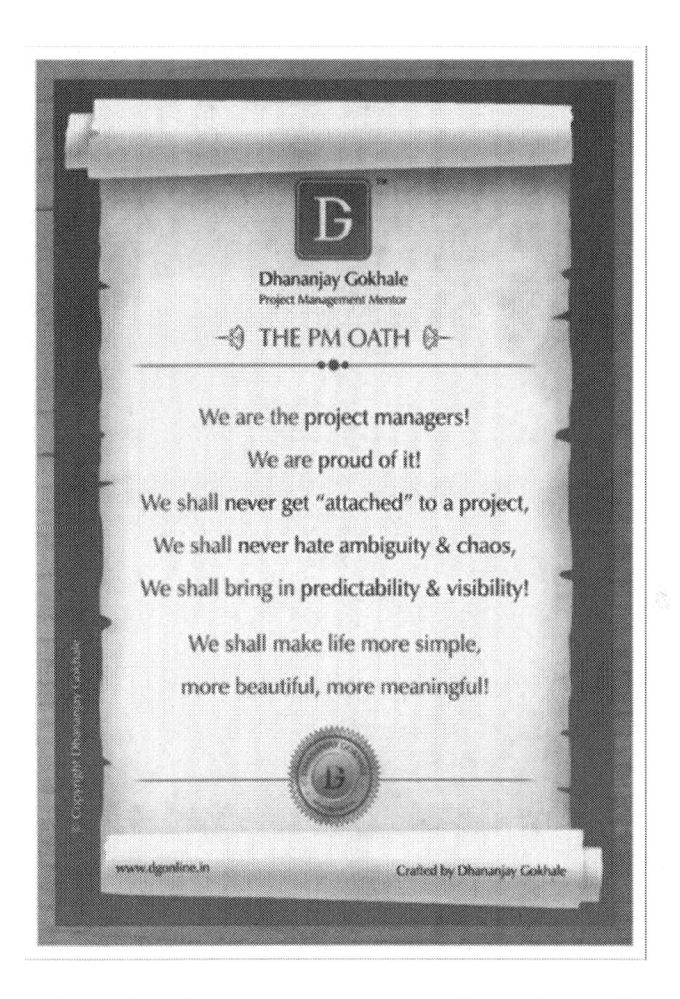

> **Dhananjay Gokhale**
> Project Management Mentor
>
> — THE PM OATH —
>
> We are the project managers!
> We are proud of it!
> We shall never get "attached" to a project,
> We shall never hate ambiguity & chaos,
> We shall bring in predictability & visibility!
> We shall make life more simple,
> more beautiful, more meaningful!
>
> www.dgonline.in   Crafted by Dhananjay Gokhale

The PM Oath guides the project manager throughout the career. It guides on four aspects.

- First, it sets the tone of appreciating the role of PM and being proud of it.
- Second, it guides on what should NOT be done.
- Third, it guide on what is to be done.
- And fourth, it constantly reminds the much higher cause or noble cause that is served by project management.

We are the project managers: We are proud of it!

Many times people don't appreciate and acknowledge that they are project managers. Anyone who is managing any project is a project manager. And one must be proud of it.

While one moves to this and starts appreciating self as a project manager, at times emotional attachment to the project strikes in. This is dangerous. And hence...,

We shall never get attached to a project!

Neither one should be indifferent to the project. The high stress levels are seen amongst project managers because of the two main reasons. Either they are very much emotionally attached to the project. Or secondly, because they do not have the temperament to sustain and tolerate ambiguity. Hence the third sentence in the oath reminds us,...

We shall never hate ambiguity & chaos.

On a lighter note, if ambiguity and chaos is absent then, project manager's job is at stake. The project managers has to navigate the project through ambiguity, chaos, assumptions, and constraints. Should the project manager be happy with it? "Not hating" is not the synonym for happy. To be happy one must understand the value of the role.

Many a times, project managers identify themselves as coordinators, communicators, etc. It is unfortunate that they do not understand the real value of project management. The real value is...

We shall bring in visibility & predictability.

Project is an endeavour that is done by, for, and of the stakeholders. There are human beings around. And a foundational instinct of a human being is "curiosity". Unmanaged curiosity leads to hostility, while well-managed curiosity leads to collaboration. The most tangible way to manage the curiosity is to bring in quantitative and reliable visibility & predictability in the everchanging environment.

Although many projects essentially done for specific customer, the most common trigger is to make the life simpler. And hence a project manager does all the tasks for basic purpose and says...

We shall make life more simple,
more beautiful,
more meaningful.

The PMO Oath

Like the PM Oath sets the guidance for project managers, the PMO Oath acts as a lighthouse for the PMO members. The PMO Oath will be appreciated only if the reader understands the meaning and context of the PM Oath. Therefore, now that we have understood the meaning of the PM Oath, we will be more appreciative of the PMO Oath.

The lack of positive self-image is the key challenge that a PMO member faces. Hence the PMO Oath starts with the lead line...

We are the PMO members.

This book is dedicated to setting up of sustainable contributory PMO. The key focus of the PMO is to develop the project management competency at the organizational level. While developing the competency of the project managers, it is necessary to define the mindset of the PMO member. It should be that of buddy and NOT the police. And hence the next line in the PMO Oath says...

We shall act as buddies of project, program, & portfolio managers to develop agility in actions.

The major value that a project manager adds to the organization is "quantitative, reliable visibility & predictability. It is possible only when project managers feels the dire need and intrinsic willingness for the same. The PMO's key contribution is to develop the intrinsic willingness. The next line in the PMO oath therefore reads...

We shall cultivate intrinsic willingness to bring in quantitative visibility & predictability in the endeavours.

The PMO Oath

We are the PMO members.

We shall act as buddies of project, program, & portfolio managers to develop agility in actions.

We shall cultivate intrinsic willingness to bring in quantitative visibility & predictability in the endeavours.

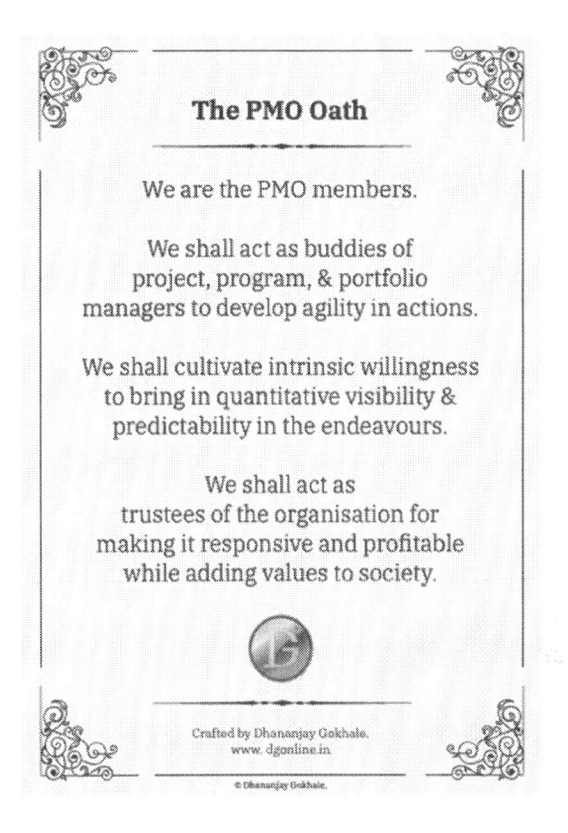

We shall act as trustees of the organisation for making it responsive and profitable while adding values to society.

Crafted by Dhananjay Gokhale.
www.dgonline.in

© Dhananjay Gokhale.

The need of the PMO is strategic. The PMO acts as an active catalytic agent in transforming the project managers, and hence transforming the organization into more responsive & more profitable in the everchanging environment.

It is said that the project manager should always take the side of the project. The project manager must remain honest to the project. The PMO helps the PM to do so. In a way the PMO acts as a trustee. The PMO is not on the leadership side, neither on the PM's side. It must act as a trustee of the organization. The decisions & contribution must always be taken keeping in mind the long term view. The PMO enables PMs, Organization Leaders, and the team! Hence the last ultimate reminder line in the PMO Oath goes as...

**We shall act as trustees of the organization
for making it responsive & profitable
while adding values to society!**

The PM Oath and PMO Oath both ultimately guide the performer to the cause of societal contribution. Each project has its impact on the society.

With these oaths let's continue our journey. I request you to keep validating the learning with the guidance in the Oaths.

Chapter 02

What Is PMO?

We are learning the concepts and implementation aspects of project and program management office set up. This learning intervention "PMO – What Works & What Doesn't?" takes you along to practically appreciate the contribution of PMO.

Let me welcome you to the 2nd chapter. The name of the Chapter is "What is PMO?"

This chapter gives you a unique perspective of PMO. There is a very rude analogy presented in this chapter. It gives the feel of 'home' to the entire endeavor. Once you are through with this chapter, your perspective of project & program management office will drastically change. You would remember this each time you enter your home.

I am sure that you would love this and would enjoy this chapter.

आश्चर्यवत्पश्यति कश्चिदेनम्
आश्चर्यवद्वदति तथैव चान्य: ।
आश्चर्यवच्चैनमन्य:शृणोति
शृत्वाप्येनं वेद न चैव कश्चित् ॥ G2.29 ॥

āshcharya-vat pashyati kaśchid enam

āshcarya-vad vadati tathaiva chānyaḥ

āshcarya-vac chainam anyaḥ shruṇoti

shrutvāpy enaṁ veda na chaiva kashchit

(Bhagwad Geeta Chater 2 - Verse 29)

What does this verse say? Some people see this as a wonder. Some people listen to it as a wonder or words come to their ears as wonder. But having gone through, have been spoken about, having expressed, none knows it at all.

Each one has one's own perspective. It is applicable to PMO as well. I love finding connects of some important aspects in Shree Bhagadwad Geeta. I did it for this concept as well. I asked myself, which shloka in Bhagvadgeeta connects to the foundational look-out to PMO? And then could find this sholka. This shloka connects to Bramhan, Aatman, or the omnipresent energy! This shloka fits to PMO as well.

I have been interviewing many people in many organizations at various levels. Especially in the context of PMO, when I ask people to describe their ideas and understanding, then each one of them narrates different perspective. Each one of them comes with different answers. It's like a story of blind men and elephant. Someone says it's a rope, other says it's a trunk. And these multiple perceptions about the PMO makes it appear as a 'wonder'.

Actually it is not so. We will have a deep dive into the PMO concepts. We can also define our own ideas about PMO. However before diving deep into the PMO concepts, I would like to present a funny analogy.

What Is PMO? | 25

Here I would like to present an analogy or a metaphor. It appears very rude. I am connecting the project & program management to roaming buffalos.

Like the buffalos that roam, project & program management is found at specific spots within the organization, as well as on the alternative grazing grounds depending on the season and the times.

The roaming buffalos! Ha..ha..!!! Isn't it funny? Isn't sarcastic? It hurts, right? Sometime this hurt helps! When the sun sets, what happens to these buffalos? Where do they go? They go back to their home, right? Why are they able to go home?

One reason is that they want to go home.

Second reason is that they are trained to go home.

And the third, most important reason is that they have a home!

And the third, most important reason is that they have a home!

Consider a case where I want to go home. I am able to go to my home but I don't have a home, then will I be able to go?

The roaming buffalos of Project & Program Management do not have a home. The PMO can take a place of home. In fact the PMO **IS** the home for the roaming buffalos of project & program management.

So in this chapter we saw that PMO appears as a wonder. Each one has his or her own perspective of PMO. And that a PMO can take place of home for the roaming buffalos of project & program management.

With this basic awareness of the minimal contribution expected from the PMO, let's now move further. The word PMO in this context represents Project & Program Management Office. However this is not only limited to management. 'Leadership' is another aspect that should be included.

Let's work on it in the next chapter.

Before moving to the next chapter, let's take a small quiz.

Mark the Statements True or False

1. PMO does not include leadership in addition to project management.

2. PMO must act as a home for project and program management.

3. PMO concept is based on individual experiences and hence appears as a 'wonder'.

4. All the people in the organization have same perspectives about PMO.

5. PMO is a department for collecting the data.

6. In reality, it is impossible to set up PMO from scratch.

Select the 2 One Right Option from a, b, c, d

7. For somebody to go home willingly, the fundamentally minimum prerequisites are all of the following except.

    a. The person should feel like going home.

    b. The person must have an owned home.

    c. The person should know how to go home.

    d. The person should have home.

For premium exclusive videos, visit https://vimeo.com/ondemand/pmowonderland or contact us at dg@dgonline.in for special discounted prices, quizzes, & 12 PDUs.

Chapter 03

P(2)M(L)O

We are learning the concepts and implementation aspects of project and program management office set up. This learning intervention "PMO – What Works & What Doesn't?" takes you along to practically appreciate the contribution of PMO.

The word PMO represents Project or Program Management Office. However this is not only limited to management. 'Leadership' is another aspect that should be included.

Let's work on it in this chapter.

Strong management with weak leadership is no better, and it sometimes actually worse than reverse.

Strong management with weak leadership is no better, and it sometimes actually worse than reverse. Isn't this a very interesting, intriguing statement? It emphasises the importance of the leadership ability and at the same times also brings in importance to the management competencies.

Who is more important – a Leader or a Manager? Gone are the days when one has a luxury to be ONLY leader or ONLY manager. Today one has to act effectively in both the roles – a leader and a manager! One has to be ambidextrous!

More precisely, P**2**MO can be a good word. P2 stands for Project & Program. The project and program managers cannot afford to be only managers. They need to develop both the competencies – Managerial competencies and Leadership competencies. They need to be **ambidextrous.**

MANAGEMENT | **LEADERSHIP**

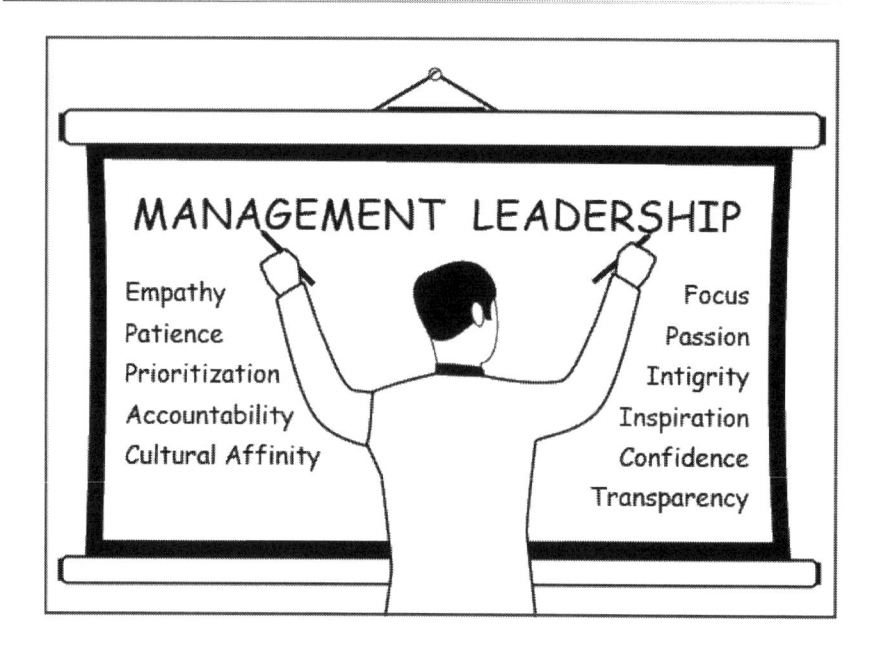

Empathy | Focus
Patience | Passion
Prioritization | Intigrity
Accountability | Inspiration
Cultural Affinity | Confidence
 | Transparency

With this perspective, P2MO should more precisely be changed to P2M**L**O – Project & Program Management and Leadership office.

---

*P2M**L**O – Project & Program Management and Leadership office.*

To maintain the parity of the word, we would use the term PMO throughout this learning intervention. Remember that, in this learning intervention, PMO it means Project & Program Management & Leadership Office.

Now, let's go to the basic question –"Why do we need leaders for Project & Program?" >>

"Why do we need leaders for projects & programs?"

I have a suggestion here. Let's take a pause here for 3 minutes. There will be silence. List at least 5 to 6 answers to the question – "why do we need leaders for projects & programs?"

We need leaders for projects & programs.

- To facilitate communication and an exchange of information among customers, suppliers, and team members in project settings.
- To gain input and commitment from team members, customers, and suppliers in developing the project vision.
- To seek innovative solutions to customer problems.
- To increase autonomy and participation of team members in project planning, decision making, problem solving, and team management.
- To establish new standards and norms for excellence in performance and productivity.
- To advance and use technology to increase productivity and performance.
- To restructure the organizational hierarchy so that work is accomplished collaboratively by means of ad hoc, temporary, and cross-functional teams.
- To promote a team culture that is consistent with restructured organizational hierarchies.
- To promote an atmosphere of trust.

To summarize, we need leaders for projects & programs for...

- Communication facilitation.
- Commitment to project vision.
- Innovation.
- Autonomy and participation.
- Excellence in performance.
- Collaborative atmosphere.

- Team culture.
- Atmosphere of trust.

While it is necessary to establish a direction and to motivate people to follow that direction, it is equally important to plan goals & to set budget; to monitor results & to look for deviations and control them.

While it is necessary to inspire trust and commitment from project teams; it is equally essential to administer, organize, and staff divisions & time throughput!

It will be easier if we understand the crossover of the competencies between a Leader & a Manager. Leader cannot afford to say – "its not my job". And hence a leader as a manager…

- Administers, organizes, and staffs division.
- Plans goals and sets budgets.
- Monitors results, looks for deviations.
- Asks "How?" and "When?"
- Maintains the status quo.
- Looks for immediate results.

Similarly a manager cannot afford to say – "its not my job". And hence a manager as a leader…

- Establishes direction and motivates people to follow that direction.
- Inspires trust and commitment from project teams.
- Fosters proactive approach amongst team members.
- Challenges the status quo.
- Sees people as dynamic, evolving resources.
- Innovates.

So coming back to the statement – Strong management with weak leadership is no better, and it sometimes actually worse than reverse. Hence it would be better called as Project and Program Management & Leadership Office.

In this chapter we appreciated the need for ambidexterity – using management & leadership. We enlisted the functions of a manager that a leader should do and vice versa.

Now to appreciate the contributions of the PMO, we must understand the basics of Project Management. The next chapter covers the basics of Project Management.

Before moving to the next chapter, let's take a small quiz.

Mark the Statements True or False

1. Strong management with weak leadership is no better, and it sometimes actually worse than reverse.
2. P2MLO stands for Project & Program Management & Leadership Office.
3. Leadership and management, both the competencies are essential for PMO.
4. PMO facilitates and builds autonomy instead of dictatorship.
5. Leader and manager activities are overlapping and must be considered together instead of in silos.
6. Goal setting and budgeting are included in management role and are not leader's jobs.
7. Seeking the innovative solutions to the stakeholder problems is included in leadership role.
8. 'To promote an atmosphere of trust' is not a function of the leadership role.
9. To establish new standards and norms for excellence in performance and productivity is not included in leadership role.
10. PMO should not focus or care about the innovation. It is part of research & development department.
11. Leader answers "What and when?", while manager answers "Why?"

Select the One Right Option from a, b, c, d

12. Which of the following are required for setting up strong PMO.

    a. Strong Management support.

    b. Leadership Skills.

    c. Large Organization.

    d. a and b.

    e. a and c.

13. Manager's role include,

    a. Perform Communication.

    b. Get commitment and support.

    c. Team coordination efforts.

    d. All of the above.

14. Functions of leader are,

    a. Focused on providing support, vision, and structure.

    b. Promote culture of trust.

    c. Provide standards.

    d. a and b.

For premium exclusive videos, visit https://vimeo.com/ondemand/pmowonderland or contact us at dg@dgonline.in for special discounted prices, quizzes, & 12 PDUs.

Chapter 04

The Basics of PM

We are learning the concepts and implementation aspects of project and program management office set up. We have travelled 3 chapters by now. We have seen the wonder perspective, roaming buffaloes, and need for ambidexterity!

Let me welcome you to the 4th chapter. **What is PM!**

This chapter forms the basis to appreciate the value addition of PMO. As we will see later, PMO must add different set of values to organization's project & program management competencies. If one needs to understand PMO's contribution, it is essential to know the project & program management to its basic form.

This chapter has the most number of animations. Hey I am not pulling the strings! ☺. You would start enjoying the game of nouns and verbs and pulling strings!!!

Someone said that...

> *"Project & Program Management is*
> *neither a rocket science nor any serious affair.*
> *It is simple, sincere, and dedicated efforts to*
> **bring in the** *quantitative visibility & predictability*
> *in an endeavour that is performed in the*
> *ever-changing environment for the benefit*
> *of the stakeholders' community"*.

No one else has said this, it is me – DG – Dhananjay Gokhale – who has said this. However unless I had begun with the lead line – "Someone said that...," you would not have paid attention to what is being said! That's the gimmick. Isn't it?

Well, all the learning interventions that I facilitate are developed based on this foundational belief of simplicity & quantitative visibility & predictability!

All the consulting and handholding assignment that I undertake are done to promote simplicity necessary to build quantitative visibility & predictability!

Program and Project Management competency build up assignments that I execute are also based on this foundational principle. The important words here are **'quantitative visibility & predictability'**.

One needs to understand that it is the matter of dealing with stakeholders. They are human beings. And the fundamental basic instinct of an every human being is **curiosity.**

When curiosity is not managed well it ultimately leads to frustration and non-collaborative atmosphere.

Whereas when this curiosity is managed well, the resistance of the people is reduced and it helps bringing collaborative atmosphere. And hence, Bringing **quantitative visibility & predictability** is the basic necessity.

Let's imagine one case. You are managing a project. You are also maintaining **quantitative visibility & predictability.** You become aware that one of the intermediate milestones would be slipped by 15 days. Once you get to know this; your first desire is to bring the date back to the expected one. Isn't it? And then starts the chain of actions. What all actions are possible?

You increase the resources, ask them to work extra, you might take help from vendors, or you might even communicate with the key stakeholders about the expected delay, you might decide to reduce the scope of the deliverables and phase out some in the next date, and many times you may cut quality as well. So what is happening here? Balancing or Compromising?

Art of balancing or compromising?

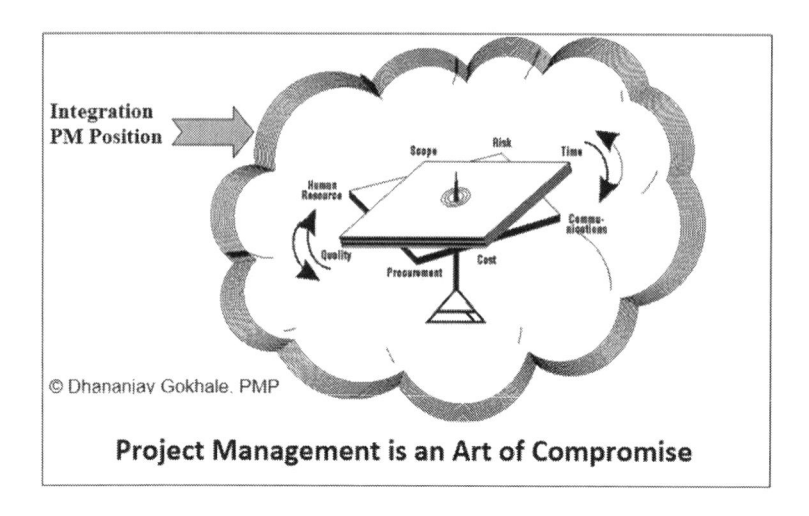

Project Management is an Art of Compromise

The project & program management is an art of balancing. More truly, it is an art of compromise – ☺ – to an extent that the person compromising should not feel that it is being done. And hence we are open to both the words. Here the word "compromise" does not bring in any negative energy.

To balance something you have to press something, you have to push something.

Here are the two planes with 4 vertices, namely Scope, Time Cost, and Quality on one plane; while HR, Communication, Risk and Procurement on the other. IN the example in the earlier parameter, the time vertex has moved from its position. And the actions suggested were on the remaining vertices. So either by pulling or pushing the other vertices, one tries to get the 'time' vertex back in the position. The PM needs to maintain the horizontal equilibrium of the planes by pulling the strings of initiating, planning, executing, monitoring & controlling, and closing.

While doing so the project or the program manager should not put own weight on the planes. A project or a program manager should be over and above the duo of these planes. Else manager's own weight would damage the equilibrium of the planes. PM should be **emotionally un-attached** to the project. Do you remember the PM Oath? Correct. It says that 'We shall never get attached to a project'. You will now be able to appreciate the importance of emotional un-attachment.

Many times, this perspective is missed and hence the emotional un-attachment is not seen. A manager who is expert in finance, starts demanding more reports and more data on the financial side. A program manager expert in law, starts focusing more on the legal side of the program. A project manager expert in technology starts focusing more on the technical aspects. This is not bad; however while doing this the key focus on project & program management is should never be lost.

How can we do it? How can we balance the two planes? How can we bring in visibility and predictability? Where do the answers for these two "ilities" lie? Where can one find them? It is a game of Questions and Answers. It is a game of Verbs and Nouns. Let's see how it works!

As a good project manager, I need to keep asking and answering these questions. And as a program manager, I must mentor my project managers to do so!

- Why & whether to do?
- What & How SHOULD happen?
- What and how is happening?
- What should vs What is?
- What and How would happen?
- Is Corrective and/or then preventive action(s) necessary?
- And, the last question is, what happened?

42 | Wonderland of PMO

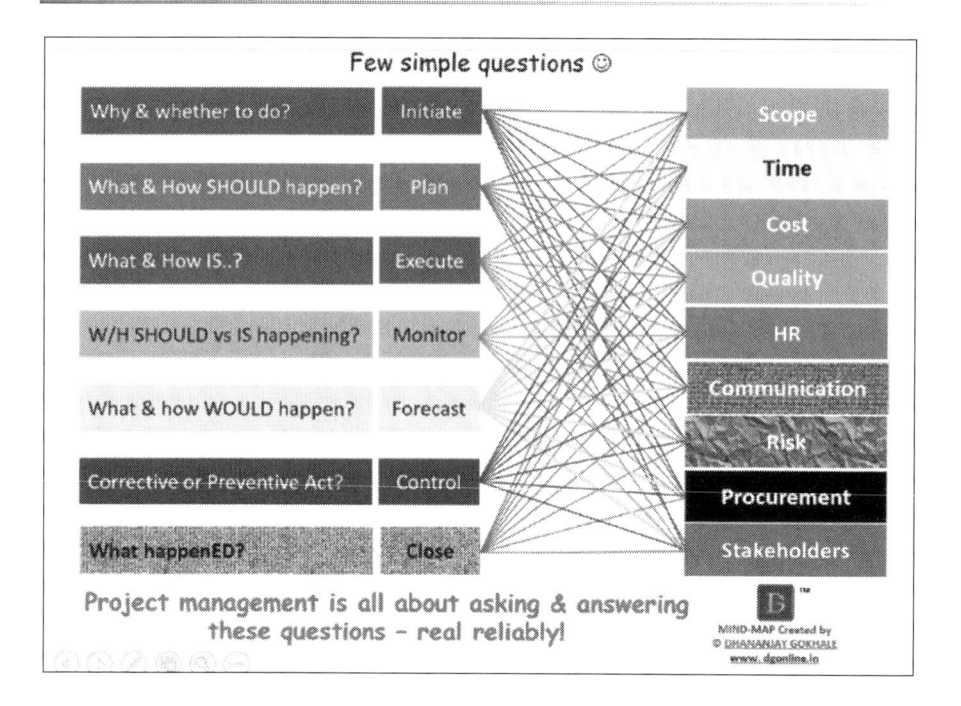

Few simple questions ☺

Questions	Verbs	Nouns
Why & whether to do?	Initiate	Scope
What & How SHOULD happen?	Plan	Time
What & How IS..?	Execute	Cost
W/H SHOULD vs IS happening?	Monitor	Quality
What & how WOULD happen?	Forecast	HR
Corrective or Preventive Act?	Control	Communication
What happenED?	Close	Risk
		Procurement
		Stakeholders

Project management is all about asking & answering these questions – real reliably!

MIND-MAP Created by
© DHANANJAY GOKHALE
www.dgonline.in

These questions when seen from the project & program management perspective, they get transformed into few verbs. These verbs are – Initiate, plan, execute, monitor, forecast, control and close. For the premium exclusive animation visit https://vimeo.com/ondemand/pmbokrevision6e/ Write to dg@dgonline.in for special discounted price for the above video.

A verb in any language acts like a force in science. As we discussed in the 3 dimensional model of project management; the focus is onto maintaining the horizontal equilibrium of the two planes. To do that we need some forces. These 7 verbs are 7 types of forces.

Each question needs to be asked in the context of each noun. There shall therefore be 63 combinations possible of these 7 verbs and 9 nouns. Those are the threads shown in the Exhibit 2 above. **Each thread represents and action.** The thread is conjunction of Verb <-> Noun.

E.g. assume, that I am managing a small (?☺) & simple (?☺) project of Passing PMP® Examination. I am a project manager and should seek the quantitative answers for a question – "What is happening?" on each area. Following is an example of questions and answers!

So, **what is happening on...?**

Scope?	PMI Membership is sought. 35 Contact Hours workshop is 50% done. In self-study, 3 processes are understood thoroughly. 25 questions are solved as a practice.
Time?	7 days are over.
Cost?	INR 15000/– paid.
Quality?	Facilitation specifications are achieved. My self-study quality in terms of focus on the subject matter is 7 on the scale of 10. Mock questions – first set of 10 questions were not ok as they were not at par with PMI standards. Later 25 were perfect.
HR?	Two people are not performing as per the responsibilities. Rest all are ok on their work.
Communication?	2 issues on communication reported. Rest communications are taking place.
Risk?	7 Risks are identified. Response actions are being taken on 3 prioritized risks.
Procurement?	2 SOWs sent. 1 contract finalized for transport for group study. Could not start drafting of the 4th SOW.
Stakeholders?	2 stakeholders added. 1 moved.

The above table is a sample example. It is mainly to elaborate how each question needs to be answered in all 9 contexts.

So now one can more systematically understand the responsibilities or actions that a competent project manager should do. The vertices of the planes are the nouns. Each of the 7 forces can act on each of the vertices. A connect of a verb to noun is an activity. So in turn a project or the program manager work on 9 * 7 = 63 activities. There shall be sixty three of them. This is all to satisfy the curiosity of the human beings involved. The verbs Monitor and Forecast, bring in Visibility and Predictability.

> *The verbs Monitor and Forecast, bring in Visibility and Predictability.*

In this chapter we saw the 3-dimentional model of project management. We enlisted 7 verbs and 9 nouns creating the ties of 63 strings. With this fundamental understanding of the 63 key actions; we will be able to appreciate the existence or the need of PMO. We can now move for understanding the basic concept of PMO.

Before that, let's take the oath once again

I crafted this Oath in the year 2007–08. I always wonder that every other profession has the professional Oath. It is the project & program management profession that does not have any Oath. And hence I decided to craft it. Many people have liked. Many have written to me that the Oath has helped them in tough situations.

Let's take the oath.

> *We are the project managers.*
> *We are proud of it.*
> *We shall never get attached to a project.*
> *We shall never hate ambiguity and chaos.*
> *We shall bring in quantitative visibility & predictability.*
> *We shall make life more simple, more beautiful, more meaningful!*
> *– Dhananjay Gokhale.*

You can also download this oath from our website www.dgonline.in Thank you all. **And, now let's move to next the topic – "What is PMO" – in our next chapter.**

Before moving to the next chapter, let's take a small quiz.

Mark the Statements True or False

1. Project Management brings in the visibility and predictability in the project in order to satisfy stakeholders' curiosity.

2. Compromise in project may be good and is required in order to bring in visibility and predictability in the continuously changing project environment.

3. PM must have a sense of possessiveness to the project.

Select the One Right Option from a, b, c, d

4. PMO or P2MLO should be

    a. In project equilibrium.

    b. Emotionally un-attached to the project.

    c. Out of individual project to be neutral.

    d. a and b.

5. The question like What should vs What is focuses on

    a. Monitoring the project.

    b. Comparing project plan vs project execution.

    c. Emphasizing on goals and objectives.

    d. a and b.

6. Project management includes actions described in following verbs:

    a. Visualize, Execute, Monitor, Control, Forecast.

    b. Initiate, Communicate, Execute.

    c. Visualize, Forecast, Demonstrate.

    d. Act, Review, Supervise.

7. Project management areas described as nouns include:

   a. Stakeholders, Communications, Human Resource.

   b. Scope, Time, Cost.

   c. Quality, Risk, Procurement.

   d. All of the above.

8. The question "Why and Whether to do?" in the context of PM means

   a. Initiating the project.

   b. Planning the project.

   c. Executing the project.

   d. Monitoring the project.

9. The question "What should happen?" in the context of PM means

   a. Initiating the project.

   b. Planning the project.

   c. Executing the project.

   d. Monitoring the project.

10. The question "What is happening?" in the context of PM means

    a. Initiating the project.

    b. Planning the project.

    c. Executing the project.

    d. Monitoring the project.

11. The question "What should happen VS what is happening?" in the context of PM means

    a. Monitoring the project.
    b. Forecasting the project.
    c. Controlling the project.
    d. Closing the project.

12. The question "What would happen?" in the context of PM means

    a. Monitoring the project.
    b. Forecasting the project.
    c. Controlling the project.
    d. Closing the project.

13. The question "DO we need to take corrective action?" in the context of PM means

    a. Monitoring the project.
    b. Forecasting the project.
    c. Controlling the project.
    d. Closing the project.

14. The question "What happened?" in the context of PM means

    a. Monitoring the project.
    b. Forecasting the project.
    c. Controlling the project.
    d. Closing the project.

15. The visibility & the predictability that one needs to bring in should be

    a. Qualitative.

    b. Detailed.

    c. Quantitative.

    d. Elaborative.

16. The visibility is connected to the verb

    a. Plan.

    b. Execute.

    c. Forecast.

    d. Monitor.

17. The predictability is connected to the verb

    a. Plan.

    b. Forecast.

    c. Monitor.

    d. Control.

18. The fundamental basic instinct of the stakeholders that must be taken care to avoid the problems in the project

    a. Curiosity.

    b. Drive for learning.

    c. Strength.

    d. Food.

For premium exclusive videos, visit https://vimeo.com/ondemand/pmowonderland or contact us at dg@dgonline.in for special discounted prices, quizzes, & 12 PDUs.

Chapter 05

PM and PMO

We are learning the concepts and implementation aspects of project and program management office set up. We have travelled 4 chapters by now. We have seen the wonder perspective, roaming buffalos, need for ambidexterity and we have also pulled 63 strings!

Let me welcome you to the 5th chapter: **A PM, & a PMO!**

It will be better if we identify the basic contributory difference between PM and PMO. In this chapter, we shall validate the focus of PMO. We will appreciate the difference between the mindsets of Project & Program Management and that of PMO.

The basic Project & Program Management will ask and will get the answer to the question "How can we get this project done effectively?" Whereas, a PMO asks, "How can we make the business more adaptive?" This is the basic difference.

The focus, thus changes from making a project or a program successful to making the business successful while achieving its set goals.

Business does not mean only money. It also means relationships, growth, development, contribution to society, and many more such aspirations. In short each institution will have its vision, mission, own goals and set of objectives. To achieve these goals, there needs a set of projects & programs. Hence it leads to multi-project, multi-program environment.

Profit means return from investment. Measurement of profit depends on the objective or the goal of the business. If the goal of my business is happiness, then profit measurement should be in terms of happiness and it should be more. If I am expecting wellness, then it should be profitable in terms of wellness.

For a person or for an institution it will be a multi project – multi program environment. Each project needs to be successfully completed. Some of these projects are independent while some of these projects are dependent on each other making a program out of it.

And hence the question that PMO asks is "How can we make the business more productive, more responsive, and thus more profitable in a rapidly changing multi-project environment?"

The answer to the above question lies in two distinct concepts. One is Project-Program Success and second is Project-Program Management Success are two distinct terms.

What is the difference? Let's see that!

A movement from Project & Program Management to PMO; crosses through very essential aspect of Project & Program Management Success. Project & Program Management success is related to project & program success; however it is NOT the same. A project or a program can be successful without the Project & Program Management success. It would be possible once or twice. However it would not be possible to achieve project & program success repeatedly if the Project & Program Management is not successful.

It needs the appreciation on the parts of all the related stakeholders. Appreciation for the systematized approach towards managing projects and programs. This again leads to the necessity of the existence of PMO. PMO ensures the existence and sustenance of Project & Program Management success.

One needs to understand that for a business to be successful, ultimately, we need to develop the project and program management competency. Project & Program Management Office – PMO – fundamentally focuses on this integrated holistic perspective.

PM and PMO | 51

Unfortunately, very few leaders understand this connect of Project – Program Management; PMO and Organization.

Project & Program and PMO are inseparable! Project & Program Management and the PMO are not exclusive islands. They are integrated interdependent entities. PM's success is PMO's success. A PMO cannot be successful unless PM is successful and so is the converse. Hence for organization's success both are needed.

Even then some leaders have a tendency to get the things done for the name sake. Let's see a real example.

Once a senior leader of a very well-known, highly certified, reputed organization was pressing hard on completing the PMO set up activity 'quickly'. I was surprised to see his behaviour. It was extremely evident that he is trying to get the things done for the namesake. Of course I appreciate his honesty in accepting the fact that he needed to show the existence of PMO because it is required for a new customer.

This is my response to that senior leader's request to set up the PMO quickly – within 3 months.

"I really appreciate your expectations of setting up the PMO in 3 months. Unfortunately, it is not possible by any means anywhere, if you are sincerely looking forward for setting up the contributory PMO. However, if you want the PMO for 'name-sake', then it is possible – even in much lesser time☺"

Setting up the PMO for name-sake does not need even one week's time. However, it is not the name-sake existence that we look forward. We look forward for PMO's performance, PMO's contribution to the business and PMO's sustainability. The PMO should serve its purpose. Then what it needs is a big organizational change. The change in the mind-set of the relevant stakeholders. It cannot happen within 3 months. We can achieve few basic milestones in 3 months, however that cannot be mistaken as functioning PMO.

Secondly, the most important aspect was that this leader intrinsically never wanted PMO. If the new client or the new contract would not have demanded for the functioning PMO; this person would not have gone for it. What he wanted was "A Name Sake PMO..."! Hence my response was – it takes less that one day to set up the PMO.

Let's understand few characteristics of the 'Name-sake' PMO.

Before moving to the next chapter, let's take a small quiz.

Mark the Statements True or False

1. Project Management and Program Management are synonyms and can be used interchangeably.

2. Focus of project management is project objective whereas focus on PMO is business objective.

3. Program may include more than one project and operations but project may not be part of any program.

4. "How can we make the business more productive?" is the underline drive for the PMO.

5. Project success can be measured only in terms of monetary profits made.

6. Program Success & Program Management Success are similar.

7. Reliability in project success is the basic output of the project management success.

8. Overall business success is a broader concept and depends on all the projects and programs in an institution.

9. Project and program management is a competency itself and should be developed in order to have sustainable success.

10. Project-Program Management and PMO are two distinct entities and hence should operate separately.

11. When the leader or a strategic sponsor intrinsically does not want PMO establishment, then what gets established is Name-sake PMO.

For premium exclusive videos, visit https://vimeo.com/ondemand/pmowonderland or contact us at dg@dgonline.in for special discounted prices, quizzes, & 12 PDUs.

Chapter 06

The Name-Sake PMO

We are learning the concepts and implementation aspects of project and program management office set up. We have travelled 4 chapters by now. We have seen the wonder perspective, roaming buffalos, need for ambidexterity and we have also pulled 63 strings! We focused on the fundamental connection between project & program management with PMO in the earlier chapter. We saw one real life example of a senior leader demanding the PMO set-up for the name-sake.

Let me welcome you to the 6th Chapter. **The Name-Sake PMO!** Understanding of the characteristics of the namesake PMO is essential. It will help us understanding & appreciating the characteristics of the **contributory PMO.**

Hence, let's understand the characteristics of the name-sake PMO in this chapter.

Vision of name-sake PMO: The 1st characteristic of the name-sake PMO is a flashy Vision. Each endeavour has its own vision. The way one sees the way one gets! **"Some said PM, some said O'PM so let's say PM'O"** is the only perspective behind a namesake PMO. It is seen as more of a new, attractive, eye-catching, & ear soothing 3 letter word. It is the mind-set of coining the new attractive words and make use of them for glamorous presentations and board room talks. If you ask a question "what and how do you define the PMO and what is the exact benefit that you want to seek?" to these leaders, then, they do not have the answer.

We discussed many aspects of the PMO in the earlier chapters. The PMO is an entity that works for making the business more responsive and more profitable. However this is never understood when one has vision of name-sake PMO.

Value Proposition: "Something 'new', 'exciting' or an additional 3 letter word that our MD can throw (…at anyone, anywhere…), an advertisement". Like in the case that I am narrating, the leader never intrinsically wanted the PMO. The existence of a PMO for him was a hook for getting new business. The person was least bothered about the need of PMO for bringing bottom line impacts. It was mainly for advertising purpose. *"I never wanted it, I never would have gone for it, it because my client wanted me to go for it and hence I am doing it"* is the mind-set that is seen. Isn't it a sheer expression of ignorance?

Recruitment Criteria for PMO staff: The only criteria is "Those people who have nothing else to do". I have seen practically that people do not want to join the PMO. The major reason is the reputation of the PMO.

With such a name-sake vision; it is but natural that people will try to keep themselves away from something that doesn't hold any value to the top management. Obviously the idea behind getting the people working for PMO merely remains at "filling the vacancies". In such case the best candidate would always be the one who doesn't have anything else to do and who cannot do anything else.

Hidden agenda of people joining: People still join the PMO, and hence, one has to check their hidden agenda. Most of the time it is to "Relax", or to Avoid travel, or to avoid pressures and politics. All these aspects are related to each other. The vision sets the value proposition. The value proposition sets the aspirations. Since the vision is name-sake, the value proposition is also for the name-sake and hence it attracts only those people who have nothing else to do or who do NOT want to do anything.

These are my personal experiences. I get many calls from many people regarding their personal and professional problems.

Once I got a call. "*DG, I am fed up of delivery pressures, travel and late night long hours working; and hence I have opted for the PMO's position in our organization. Can you help me in preparing for the interview?*" I think this questions explains everything.

People confidently feel that the PMO is a place for relaxation because no one would really bother about who does what, when and how.

People confidently feel that the PMO is a place for relaxation because no one would really bother about who does what, when and how.

It is definitely true in case of the name-sake PMO. The way you sow the way you reap. Isn't it? There is a very evident reason behind it that is mentioned in the next parameter.

Reporting to: God! Only God knows to whom the name-sake PMO would report to.

> *Only God knows to whom the name-sake PMO would report to.*

PMO is a strategic initiative. It should be owned by the key leadership. And hence must be reporting into the strategic leadership. However the vision and the value proposition at the strategic leadership in the name-sake PMO creates this confusion. Do you think that the leader who wrote to me about his wish of getting the PMO set up for the sake of client requirement, would ever own the PMO? Would that person take the comprehensive accountability of setting up the PMO? And hence it is always a confusion about the reporting relationship of the PMO. Even if there is a designated reporting place or position for a PMO, it is considered merely as head-count management.

Chart of accounts: Miscellaneous, or entertainment! A chart of accounts (COA) is a financial organizational tool that provides a complete listing of every account in an accounting system. An important purpose of a COA is to segregate expenditures, revenue, assets and liabilities so that viewers can quickly get a sense of a company's financial health. A well-designed COA not only meets the information needs of management, it also helps a business to comply with financial reporting standards. When the vision and value proposition of the namesake PMO itself is blurred, how can one expect to have a clear chart of accounts for the namesake PMO? The funding, the budget, the measurement of the performance would not exist formally. In short the namesake PMO would not have its own authentic budget. It would survive on the mercy of other chart of accounts.

Let's continue further with few more parameter with characteristics of the name-sake PMO.

60 | Wonderland of PMO

Competency Required: Excellent DTP skills (with mastery on 'ctrl-C ctrl-V) Tenacious begging capacity.

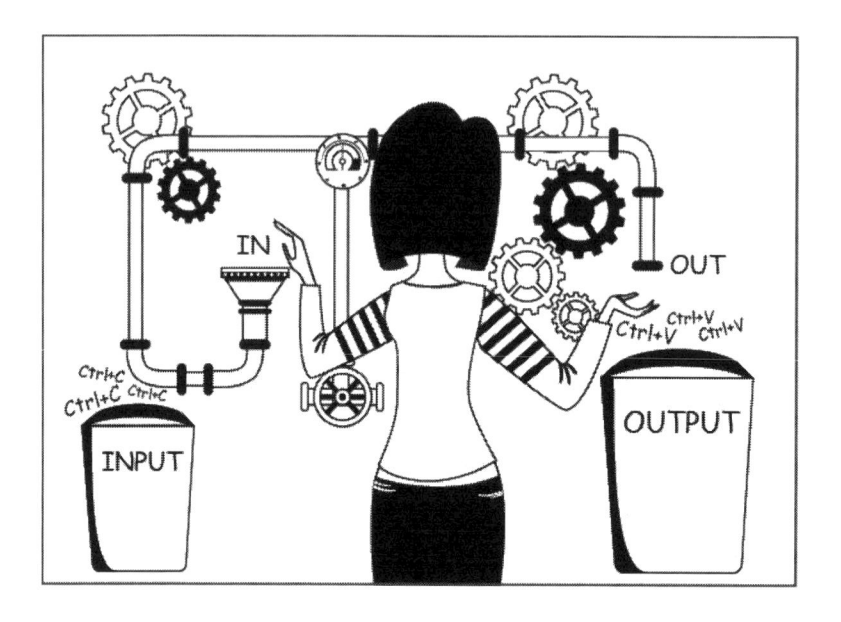

As we saw in the earlier part, the people joining the name-sake PMO are not the one who are competent for the PMO's job. Further considering the vision and the value proposition that the namesake PMO has; the competencies required are totally different than those are required for the Contributory PMO. The only job left for such namesake PMOs are preparing the presentations for the projects. The data and information in the presentation are also not intuitively collected. They are collected from the sources out of the systems. And hence most of the time, copy-paste are the operations performed by the people working in the name-sake PMO.

So before and after every project review meeting PMO members spent huge time in preparing and manipulating the presentations, by using different attractive templates, color combinations, and images. The sad part is that the discussion mainly is concentrated on creating good feelings. The colors and look & feel seems to be more important than the reliable quantitative data.

KPAs/KRAs: Provide numerous versions in '.ppt', '.xls' w/o questioning the use with different color schemes, font size, themes.

KPA stands for Key Performance Area and KRA stands for Key Result Area. We saw in the competencies necessary to join the name-sake PMO. With such competency expectations, and with such people joining the name-sake PMO, one cannot expect any better KPA/KRA than these. The more focus is given on only preparing the presentations. The real contribution of PMO is missed.

In many of my assignments, I have observed that the responsibilities of the PMO are kept restricted to data collection and to prepare presentations. People claim that they do the analysis of the data. However if the data itself is non-quantitative and non-reliable, then how is it possible and how is useful to do any analysis. Many a times the major part of the name-sake PMO is consumed in doing calculations for generating the invoices. And hence, accurate data of the efforts, cost, time is always missing because the time sheets are adjusted according to the contractual terms.

Organizational Position: Anywhere, especially where there is maximum redundancy! We saw that one of the parameters is "Reporting Structure". There is absolutely no clarity as regards reporting of the name-sake PMO. Hence it is very difficult to formulate the organizational position of the PMO. The name-sake PMO never gets a clear place in the organization structure. It is always buried under either quality group or finance group or accounts or delivery head. Many a times the responsibilities that name-sake PMO performs are redundant. Hence the PMO members are looked upon as overheads.

Career Path: Festival Contribution Collector and or Starting Roadside Printing Business! Another very important parameter is 'career path' for the people working in PMO. When it is a name-sake PMO, considering the competencies of the people joining, their willingness, their vested interest behind joining the PMO, and the value proposition that the organization leader sees in the name-sake PMO, the career path for the PMO members are never thought upon. On a very blackish comedy flavor, the only career that these people can do extremely well, would be – festival contribution collector. The one roams from door to door to collect the festival contribution on the mercy of the donors.

This may sound very rude, however this is the fact that I have seen in last two decades. Even today the changes are happening at extremely slow rate. The organization leaders are busy showing the mere existence than the functioning & effectiveness of PMO.

> *The organization leaders are busy showing the mere existence than the functioning & effectiveness of PMO.*

Set-up Time: Get the Pizza Free…30 minutes!! There was a television commercial about the pizza delivery. The commercial used to promise that in case the pizza doesn't get delivered in 30 minutes then the customer can get it completely free. The only reason that I am mentioning the jingle of the commercial here is that the similar promise can be made for setting up the name-sake PMO. One needs only few things to set up the name-sake PMO and those can be arranged in less than 30 minutes time.

Fate: Once upon a time! In short. The name-sake PMO does not last longer – neither from the durational nor from the contribution perspective. And hence, the people end up saying – one upon a time we tried doing it, but…!

So, these are the characteristics of Namesake PMO. With this, how can it serve the purpose of making the business more adaptive & more responsive helping organization achieving the goals? It will never be able to do that. In fact it is better **NOT** to have PMO than to have Namesake PMO.

In fact it is better <u>NOT</u> to have PMO than to have Namesake PMO.

In fact it is better NOT to have PMO than to have Namesake PMO. It will save not only the time and money of the organization; but it will also protect the organizations from the negativity generated by the namesake PMO and its members.

It was necessary to understand the characteristics of the name-sake PMO. We did that. So, are we expecting 'name-sake' PMO or Are we driving to set up the 'contributory' PMO?

Of course we are not expecting the name-sake PMO.

So let's understand the characteristics of the **Contributory** PMO. However before identifying and listing them, let's first graphically understand the PMO.

Before moving to the next chapter, let's take a small quiz.

Mark the Statements True or False

1. PMO is contributory when it has a defined committed vision.

2. PMO competencies includes leadership skills and it should be reported to organizational leadership in order to implement in most contributory way.

3. PMO is only namesake if it does not serve the value proposition that it should.

4. An important purpose of a Chart of Account is to segregate expenditures, revenue, assets and liabilities so that viewers can quickly get a sense of a company's financial health.

Select the One Right Option from a, b, c, d

5. Recruiting staff for Name-sake PMO is challenging due to

    a. Vaguely defined job description.

    b. Reputation of PMO.

    c. Mind-set for PMO job.

    d. All of the above.

6. Mostly people join PMO job as it is considered to be

    a. Low on workload and pressure.

    b. More onsite opportunities.

    c. Highly paid.

    d. All of the above.

7. Confusion about PMO account is about

    a. Finance requirement.

    b. Chart of Account.

c. Funding policies.

d. All of the above.

8. Value Proposition of the Name sake PMO is

    a. Interesting 3 letters word.

    b. Nothing else to do.

    c. To relax, To avoid travel.

    d. Miscellaneous.

9. Recruitment Criteria of the Name sake PMO is

    a. Interesting 3 letters word.

    b. Nothing else to do.

    c. To relax, To avoid travel.

    d. Miscellaneous.

10. Hidden agenda of people joining of the Name sake PMO is

    a. Interesting 3 letters word.

    b. Nothing else to do.

    c. To relax, To avoid travel.

    d. Miscellaneous.

11. Chart of accounts of the Name sake PMO is

    a. Miscellaneous.

    b. DTP skills, begging.

    c. Anywhere.

    d. Printing business.

12. Competencies required for joining the Name sake PMO is

    a. Miscellaneous.

    b. DTP skills, begging.

    c. Anywhere.

    d. Printing business.

13. Organizational position of the Name sake PMO is

    a. Miscellaneous.

    b. DTP skills, begging.

    c. Anywhere.

    d. Printing business.

14. Career path for the members of the Name sake PMO is

    a. Miscellaneous.

    b. DTP skills, begging.

    c. Anywhere.

    d. Printing business.

For premium exclusive videos, visit https://vimeo.com/ondemand/pmowonderland or contact us at dg@dgonline.in for special discounted prices, quizzes, & 12 PDUs.

Chapter 07

4 Baskets of Contributory PMO

We are learning the concepts and implementation aspects of project and program management office set up. We have travelled 6 chapters by now. We have seen the wonder perspective, roaming buffalos, need for ambidexterity and we have also pulled 63 strings! We focused on the fundamental connection between project & program management with PMO in the earlier chapter. We saw one real life example of a senior leader demanding the PMO set-up for the name-sake. We then listed the characteristics of the name-sake PMO.

Let me welcome you to the 7th Chapter. **The 4 baskets of PMO!** It is essential to visualize the basic PMO model and the 4 baskets of support that PMO offers.

---

*PMO should gain the ability and enable the organization to answer the question "How can we make the business more adaptive, **responsive and thus more profitable in a rapidly changing multi-project environment?"***

We have seen this paradigm of PMO in our very first chapter. It calls for building the competencies. PMO should gain the ability and enable the organization to answer the question "How can we make the business more adaptive, responsive and thus more profitable in a rapidly changing multi-project environment?" It happens through very specific support provided to the organization – to the project and program managers. This support is four-fold in four baskets. 1. Library reference, 2. Mentoring & training 3. Services and 4. Strategic. We will be discussing it more specifically in the later part.

I have come to define these 4 baskets based on my experience of past decade. This concept has always helped the organizations. These 4 baskets are full of common sense. They are evolved purely out of basic needs of project and program managers if they wish to enhance their competencies. Now, let's understand how this support is connected to the organization.

Say there is an organization. Each organization has its own vision and mission, and goals. It creates different areas of work. They are also known as LOBs – Line of Business. Each line of business is a portfolio consisting operations, projects, and programs. The vision is achieved by an integrated performance of all these. There would be lot of projects and programs. Small, large, simple, medium and similar characteristics can be used to classify them.

A project manager would be appointed to manage an individual project. So there will be many projects in the organization that will be managed individually. Over a period, we would need some standard way. This will help bringing in uniformity and more importantly it will reduce or eliminate reinventing already invented wheels. It will reduce the same mistakes being done repeatedly. These will be set of templates, guidelines, past data, etc. So the project managers managing projects would be more effective.

It is not a one way traffic. Even an individual keeps contributing to the standard way. So it is a two way connection. Project & program managers make use of standard ways while contributing to them & refining them. And when these interactions happen regularly, willingly, then probably we start marching towards matured project & program management culture in the organization.

Here comes very important aspect. The aspect of prioritization. Although there exists a matured project and program management culture in the organization; if the leaders choose or prioritize non-contributing projects and program; it will be of no use, even if they complete such projects or programs successfully.

4 Baskets of Contributory PMO | 69

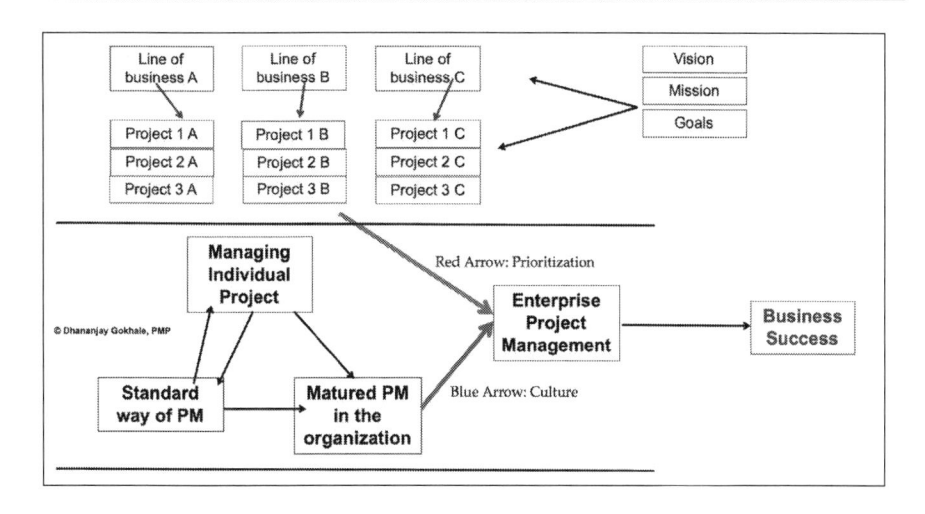

```
┌─────────────────────────────────────────────────────────────────────┐
│   Line of          Line of         Line of              Vision      │
│   business A       business B      business C                       │
│                                                         Mission     │
│   Project 1 A      Project 1 B     Project 1 C          Goals       │
│   Project 2 A      Project 2 B     Project 2 C                      │
│   Project 3 A      Project 3 B     Project 3 C                      │
│                                                                     │
│             Managing                                                │
│             Individual           Red Arrow: Prioritization          │
│             Project                                                 │
│                                  Enterprise          Business       │
│                                  Project             Success        │
│                                  Management                         │
│                                                                     │
│   Standard         Matured PM    Blue Arrow: Culture                │
│   way of PM        in the                                           │
│                    organization                                     │
└─────────────────────────────────────────────────────────────────────┘
```

Let's refer to blue and red arrow. What is blue arrow? Matured PM organization helping creating standard ways and helping managing individual projects.

What is Red arrow? It is all about prioritization. Only rightly prioritized projects & programs are done in the organization.

How many of us are aware about pet projects in the organization?

Pet projects are those projects where, this connect between project's or program's objective and the business need is not or cannot be justified.

All those projects that avoid business cases are pet projects. They don't have business case. So the existence of Red Arrow is a key success factor. It is the presence of objective prioritization. It has to be strong. Then probably we can go ahead with Enterprise Project/Program management. This leads to the success.

That's a basic **foundation** of a PMO. In short, when PMO is a Contributory PMO, then one can achieve the business success through this path. Now let's move forward to see where PMO fits into this mind-map.

"If the chief of the organization has promised to offer all kind of support then what all support do you need or expect from the organization?"

I have asked this question to many project and program managers in last two decades. Unfortunately more than 80% of the time, I got the answers like – we need money, we need more resources, we need tools, we need automation and so on.

It is like asking one cup of coffee, when the God comes and asks you what do you need?

A competent project & program manager shall demand the following:

A competent project or program manager would say, "I know my job and hence I do not expect anybody to do my job. I can do my job and I will do it. But you can tell me in case someone has done this kind of a job earlier in our organization. I would need library reference, data. I need history. I need place where I can go and search, view, watch the past projects & programs. **This forms the need for the support from the 1st – Library basket of the PMO.**

Secondly, I need somebody who can mentor me. I need someone who can train me. Because there are lots of incompetence that I have. I don't know how to write risk, I don't understand how to manage people. I don't know how to do the costing. And hence I need someone to develop me, train me, and mentor me. This will accelerate my learnings and consequently will lead the organization towards success. **This forms the need for the support from the 2nd – Mentoring/ Training basket of the PMO.**

Third, I would need some services also. There are some things that I **KNOW how to** do but I am **not able** to do. I need support from someone who can hold my hands while I do it. I will write a risk register and develop a schedule. Can someone review those and let me know areas of improvement? I might have made couple of mistakes while estimating efforts. Can someone point those for me? And let's now eliminate each mistake so that I will not make the same mistake again. This will help me increasing my competency resulting into matured PM culture in the organization. **This forms the need for the support from the 3rd – 'PM Services' basket of the PMO.**

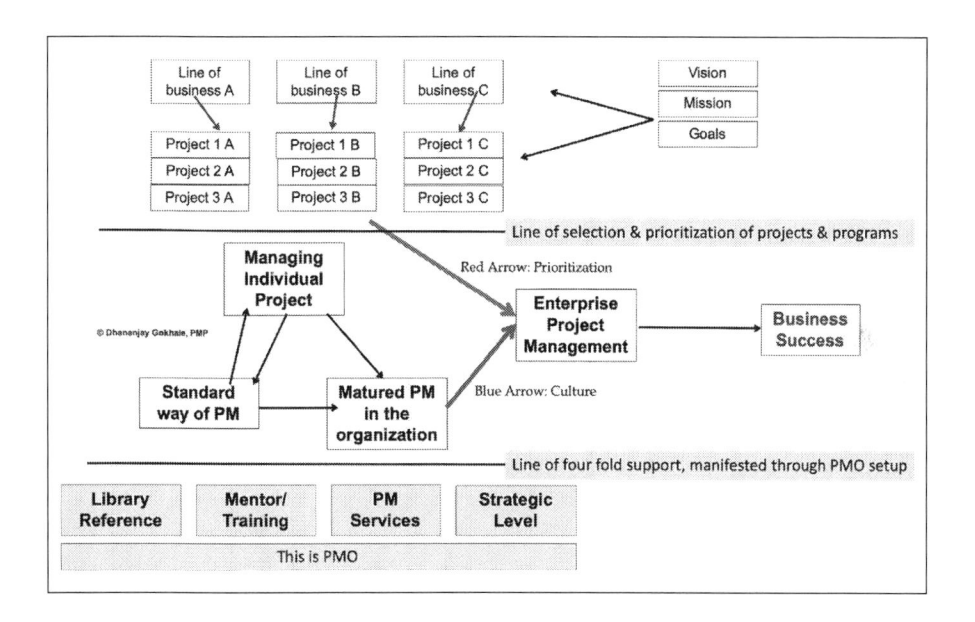

And last but definitely not the least; can I get strategic level support? If I am claiming something which people generally not very eager to hear to, would there be someone who will help me pleading this case and in the court of management? Who would like to listen to that? Would Account manager listen to that? Whom shall I go and communicate? **This forms the need for the support from the 4th – Strategic Presence basket of the PMO.**

So these are the four aspects that I need support from you. This is the answer from a matured PM. **And in short, this support is PMO. Project & Program Management & Leadership office.** So the project & program management office is not the physical room where 3 people are sitting day in and day out. It is more of the services provided.

Library Reference (L)	Mentor/ Training (M)	PM Services (P)	Strategic Level (S)
This is PMO			
Four fold support, manifested through PMO setup			

PMO: 4 Baskets

These are the four baskets where PMO constantly support the project and the program managers in the organization. It is a huge work. In the later part of this learning intervention, we will be working on how to make it happen.

However, even at this stage we are clear on some aspects. If PMO means reliable existence of these 4 baskets, then.

- Can we make it happen in 3 months? No not possible.

- Can we separate it out from PM Maturity and Organization success? No not possible.

- Can we afford to have people recruited here who want rest and leisure? No not possible.

- Can it afford to have people who have only DTP skills? No not possible.

Hence I had responded to that senior leader that 3 months are NOT necessary to set up Namesake PMO while 3 months is ¼ th of a time that one needs to set up a contributory PMO. With this clarity on the 4 areas of support, let's now move to the functions of PMO.

Before moving to the next chapter, let's take a small quiz.

Mark the Statements True or False

1. In addition to matured PM organization, it is essential to have correct prioritization of projects in program or portfolio for successful enterprise project management.

2. Those project that avoid the business case which aligns vision to project objective are known as 'pet' project.

3. Project and program manager should have right demands in order to get those fulfilled.

4. Library support offers support on past project data and history along with all the past project details.

5. PMO can be set in 3 months' time as it is just a mind-set change.

6. Project and program managers require training and mentoring from PMO to develop the competencies which will accelerate the learnings.

7. PMO is separate from PM Maturity and Organization success.

Select the One Right Option from a, b, c, d

8. Cost estimates of the past projects can be offered to Project & Program Managers through which of the 4 baskets of the PMO?

    a. Library Support.

    b. Training & Mentoring Support.

    c. PM Services Support.

    d. Strategic Support.

9. "Project Schedule Tracking Workshop" can be offered to Project & Program Managers through which of the 4 baskets of the PMO?

    a. Library Support.

    b. Training & Mentoring Support.

    c. PM Services Support.

    d. Strategic Support.

10. "Risk Register Review Workshop" can be offered to Project & Program Managers through which of the 4 baskets of the PMO?

    a. Library Support.

    b. Training & Mentoring Support.

    c. PM Services Support.

    d. Strategic Support.

11. "Project Prioritization Debate" can be offered to Project & Program Managers through which of the 4 baskets of the PMO?

    a. Library Support.

    b. Training & Mentoring Support.

    c. PM Services Support.

    d. Strategic Support.

12. A program manager wants to know the projects distribution strategies that earlier Program Managers followed. This can be offered to Project & Program Managers through which of the 4 baskets of the PMO?

    a. Library Support.

    b. Training & Mentoring Support.

c. PM Services Support.

d. Strategic Support.

13. A project manager wants someone to review the project schedule developed. This can be offered to through which of the 4 baskets of the PMO?

    a. Library Support.

    b. Training & Mentoring Support.

    c. PM Services Support.

    d. Strategic Support.

14. A project manager wants to know the buffer calculations in critical chain project management methodology. This can be offered through which of the 4 baskets of the PMO?

    a. Library Support.

    b. Training & Mentoring Support.

    c. PM Services Support.

    d. Strategic Support.

15. A program manager strongly feels that one of the projects pushed into the program does not have any connect to the program or organization business goals, vision, & strategy. The support can be offered to Program Managers through which of the 4 baskets of the PMO?

    a. Library Support.

    b. Training & Mentoring Support.

    c. PM Services Support.

    d. Strategic Support.

16. In matured project and program management, two-way information flow happens between Project and PMO for

    a. Lessons learnt.

    b. Set of guidelines and procedures.

    c. Processes, Best practices, information, and data.

    d. All of the Above.

For premium exclusive videos, visit https://vimeo.com/ondemand/pmowonderland or contact us at dg@dgonline.in for special discounted prices, quizzes, & 12 PDUs.

Chapter 08

Functions of the Contributory PMO

We are learning the concepts and implementation aspects of project and program management office set up. We have travelled 7 chapters by now.

We have seen the wonder perspective, roaming buffalos, need for ambidexterity and we have also pulled 63 strings! We focused on the fundamental connection between project & program management with PMO in the earlier chapter. We saw one real life example of a senior leader demanding the PMO set-up for the name-sake.

We then listed the characteristics of the name-sake PMO. We also elaborated the 4 baskets of PMO.

Let me welcome you to the 8th Chapter. **The functions of contributory PMO.** Now let's enlist and elaborate the functions of PMO. Later we can segregate it into the 4 baskets.

We have seen the 4 baskets of PMO. With this clarity on the 4 areas of support – Library reference, Mentoring & Training, PM Services, & Strategic Level Support, let's now move to the functions of PMO.

Function 01: Generate organization-wide awareness for maintaining the uniformity in using project management vocabulary/tools/techniques and project structure.

Let's hypothetically think that we have decided not to follow any process. Who should create this awareness? Someone should be doing that. Do you think it's a simple task to communicate with the people and tell them not to follow any process? It is definitely not. The human tendency is that to resist anything that has been told.

Then imagine the situation when we expect everyone to follow same process. How easy it would be? PMOs should be the Harbingers. They create the awareness about vocabulary, tools, techniques, guidelines, templates, and best practices related to the project & program management in the organization.

Functions of the Contributory PMO | 79

Function 02: Impart training to Project & Program Managers and Team Members on Project & Program Management tool(s)/concepts/techniques.

One must ensure that these programs must be extremely effective in terms of generating interest and willingness to learn and implement.

Creating awareness is the first step. Awareness is to be supported by interest and then information. PMO must design and deliver the training programs at all levels in the organization generating interest that will trigger **intrinsic willingness** of the organization members. **Interest generation** and **Information transfer** are the two major focus areas of the trainings in the initial phases of the development. PM Fundamentals, need for quick reviews, other areas in PM like time, scope, cost, and quality are some of the areas that I focus for development in this function.

One must ensure that these programs must be extremely effective in terms of generating interest and willingness to learn and implement.

Unfortunately I have seen many organizations where such programs are not at all given much value. Many HR and Training managers feel that such trainings can be delivered by less experienced faculty and can be of very low pricing. On the contrary, this is to be done by a very experienced facilitator who is equally skilled in PM.

Although the program duration is lesser, the value addition is tremendous. Generating the intrinsic willingness needs a creation of massive amount of interest, attraction and love for the subject.

Function 03: Third function is to compile the project MIS. This is the foundation for future actions. More reliable and accessible the data, lesser the time spent in reinvention of the wheels. The Awareness and Interest generating trainings are key contributors in generating the data. Such trainings and learning interventions create positive & receptive mindset of the people in creating the reliable data. Now when such data points are generated, then we should have a provision to record and store it. That will be a library reference for other projects and programs. Hence this data should be reliable. It should be free from biases and pressures.

E.g. if the people are pressurized to mark 8 hours in the timesheet irrespective their actual work; then we will not have the good data. We will lose on the facts. Instead, if the organization leader is matured enough to expect and motivate people to fill in the true timesheet, then we will have reliable foundations for future estimates. This attitude of respecting and hence maintaining the true data is generated by PMO. Hence PMO will initially help compiling the data for decision making.

Function 04: Conduct Post Implementation Review.

Project implementation review serves two purposes –

a. Learning and

b. Course Correction as necessary.

The review that contributes neither to learning nor to course correction, are not the reviews.

The reviews should be succinct – to the point. The review that contributes neither to learning nor to course correction, are not the reviews. ON a very lighter scale I say that those reviews which are not conducted professionally do add a value of entertainment. A project review meeting can be source of laughter, a comedy show, or a fairy tale bonanza. PMO needs to abolish this fairy tell mindset. It needs to bring in quantitative expressions in the review meetings.

PMO needs to bring in accuracy and speed in the review meetings.

An extremely matured PM culture will witness each review meeting getting over at the end of 9th minute. It is **SMRM™** – **Single Minute Review Meeting**. (SMRM is a concept developed by Dhananjay Gokhale.) The entire meeting must be done on data points. I have a list of 7 questions that one can ask and answer. If the review meeting is stretched on story telling mode, it should be curtailed. This **SMRM™** helps in increasing the frequency of such meetings. More the frequency, quicker the updates and hence quicker the course corrections as necessary. This also increases the attention and the interest of the participants.

Unfortunately, I have witnessed 1 to 1.5 hour meetings. Participants having absolutely no clue, busy yawning, or thumbing cell phones. Such review meetings have become a laughing stock and source of negative energy. People shiver and get demotivated when they get an invite of such review meetings. PMO has opportunity to turnaround this situation.

Post implementation or post project reviews should document how the life of the project was. The project has just left its body. How did it live its life? What mistakes that he has done? What good things he has done? That's why we end up reading autobiographies and biographies. It's a history of a life that was present for some years which brings in learning for others. Competent project & program manager need to write books of projects & program.

Functions of the Contributory PMO | 83

Function 05: Participate in all key planning, scheduling, and problem resolution meetings. And Evaluate proposed changes to the project plan and make recommendations.

Initially PMs and other stakeholders would hesitate to invite PMO members in the meetings. We will discuss this aspect later. Nevertheless, even if PMO members are not invited, they must be present.

One needs to understand that PMO should act as an extended brain, mind, heart and body of the project managers. PMO should help going all the way to increase the competency of Project and Program Managers. However the paradox is that the beneficiaries – i.e. the project and the program managers themselves are the resisters. They turn out to be supporters as and when they start seeing the value addition of the PMO in the four boxes of Library, Training & Mentoring, Services and Strategies as explained in the earlier contents.

It is all about the trust building movement. When PMO members attend and participate in planning, scheduling, and problem resolution meeting; more opportunities are sought to do so. PMO can bring in the value by working out 'what if…' analysis visualizing multiple scenarios. This enriches the efficiency of the decisions.

Function 06: Provide an independent view of the status of the project(s) to the senior management.

The mindset of the PMO should be that of trustee. PMO should not take anybody's side. It is easier said than done. Many times, I have seen, that in the race of popularity, PMO members either start taking side of project & program managers or senior management. There are incidences where I have witnessed few PMO members playing double agent. They take side of project & program managers and also that of senior management conveniently.

Supporting some body and taking side of someone are totally different perspectives. The focus of the PMO is to make the organization more adaptive & responsive in the changing environment achieving its goal and vision. So if at all, PMO takes any side, then it would be of this guiding principle and none else. This needs developing the competencies at all levels in the organization – project & program managers, their 2nd in commands, team members, senior managers, strategic sponsors, and many more.

Providing independent view on the project & program helps senior management taking decisions. It also brings about the holistic view about the organization in adapting this cultural change. The PMO should also raise red flags when any problems are foreseen by providing an independent assessment of the situation.

Function 07: Provide ongoing assistance to project & program managers in project management activities.

This function contributes to "service" box. Competency comprises of 3 aspects – knowledge, skills and attitudes. The work of PMO starts with one (or very few) project & program managers. We will discuss this aspect in detail when we will work on actions for setting up the PMO. These very few project or program managers are those rare species who have the ability to understand the contribution of the PMO. They are willing to get support from the PMO. Amongst them, few are knowledgeable. They are aware about few principles of the project and program management. These rare of rare people need support on skill development.

For example, a supportive project manager knows the importance of robust schedule development. However, that person cannot develop such a schedule using the tool prescribed in the organization, say Microsoft Project. This is where PMO should jump in and bridge the gap between knowledge and skills of the interested project managers. This should not be a onetime activity.

The idea is to make such people mentors in the skills. This job of PMO does not end with one or two project managers. Seeing the benefits that these people receive due to involvement of PMO, other 'on the fence' project & program managers also start approaching the PMO. The services offered by a PMO may vary like – helping PM in schedule development, doing reviews of the risk register developed by the PM, helping PMs in estimations, helping PMs in validations and reviews of the estimates, helping PMs performing what if analysis for corrective actions, etc. We have already discussed this part in the topic of – 4 baskets of PMO.

Function 08: Explore newer project management tools, concepts and methodologies.

The terms 'new' and 'old' are subjective. Imagine an organization, where no project or program manager uses schedule. They are not even aware about developing and tracking the schedule. Simple concepts of activity sequencing and drafting them on board would be a new tool for them. Once the people understand the advantages in this, they can be taken to critical path methodology.

Critical Chain CCPM method evolved in late 90s. Wasn't it new then for those who have reached the maturity in critical path methodology. There are few organizations where this is a brand new concept even today. There are project and program managers today who have not even heard about this concept, let apart the implementation.

There should be a drive for continuous improvement maintained by the PMO by continuously researching the new concepts – new to the world and/or new to the organization.

As we said, PMO needs to bring up the Leadership competencies as well, because, Project and program management needs leadership competencies. Hence the research should be done in both management and leadership arena.

Function 09: Coordinate project activities across the organizations.

This is equally important function that a PMO should perform. While the PMO needs to develop the project and program management competency, it is extremely important to pay attention to other organization functions including other project verticals.

I always suggest to start slow. Focus only on selected 2 to 3 projects and build on them. Even if the PMO pays attention to few select project, it has to pay attention to across organization in the context of those. For example, purchase department, or IT department, or R&D department needs to appreciate the project and program activities synchronization. I many times facilitate "Project Management for Support Groups" workshop.

Function 10: Here comes an amazing function – Act as a Simulator!!!

Now a question to you: How does a doctor, a chartered accountant, a lawyer, or a flight pilot gets a permission to perform their jobs? Each one of then needs to hold a specific educational qualification, a formal education in their field. Later, more importantly, each one of them has to undergo an article ship or an internship or an apprenticeship under the guidance of an expert while serving as an assistant. In fact, it is a mandate.

How about a project or a program manager? Is there any apprenticeship mandated for them?

Have you seen a simulator that can provide this contribution for Project & Program Management somewhere?

It is only the PMO who can serve as a simulator.

It is the senior leadership team who needs to mandate that each project and program manager must work in PMO for at least 8 to 10 months. When one works under PMO, that person will end up doing all the activities in all the 4 buckets of PMO that we have discussed. The person gets tremendous exposure. Further PMO does not have delivery pressures. Hence these people will be able to focus more attention to their learnings and grasping. Although the PMO members are not accountable to delivery, they need to support the project and program managers thoroughly.

Have you seen a simulator that can provide this contribution for Project & Program Management somewhere? It is only the PMO who can serve as a simulator. PMO could be a wonderful simulator. An individual gets an exposure of at least 6 years in a span of 1 year. Why? In one year the person sees at least 6 to 10 projects. And you contribute in those projects & programs as if they are yours. You work with them. An individual gets a chance to work with experts. You put your heart, brain, body into them and as a result your competencies are increased. So that's a simulator. So it is a good idea that before asking anybody to be a project or program manager, ask that person to work under PMO for at least 6 to 8 months. Budding project and program managers should definitely spend time in PMO.

Function 11: And last and the most important – Develop organizational PM competency! We shall dwell upon this **in our next chapter.**

Before moving to the next chapter, let's take a small quiz.

Mark the Statements True or False

1. Compiling project MIS is required for making future decisions.

2. Post–implementation reviews may not be required as project is already over.

3. PMO can add value in review meeting by minimizing the meeting time and maximizing the value-add.

4. PMOs are Harbingers as they create awareness about vocabulary, tools, techniques, guidelines, templates, and best practices.

5. A thorough retrospect of each project should be documented and it is part of post-project tasks of PMO.

6. PMO should act as non-biased trustee.

7. PMO should provide independent reviews but should not raise any red flags or concerns as it is not its job.

8. The initial training programs must have detailed course coverage.

9. Simulator action is to provide a chance to practically use the attained knowledge and skills.

10. The concept SMRM™ developed by Dhananjay Gokhale stands for Single Minute Review Meeting.

Select the One Right Option from a, b, c, d

11. The PMO function – 'Generate organization-wide awareness' falls into which of the 4 baskets?

    a. Library reference.

    b. Training & mentoring.

    c. PM Services.

    d. Strategic Support.

12. The PMO function – 'Develop uniform vocabulary' falls into which of the 4 baskets?.

    a. Library reference.

    b. Training & mentoring.

    c. PM Services.

    d. Strategic Support.

13. The PMO function – 'Develop and support on new tools and techniques' falls into which of the 4 baskets?

    a. Library reference.

    b. Training & mentoring.

    c. PM Services.

    d. Strategic Support.

14. The PMO function – 'Develop organizational PM Competency' falls into which of the 4 baskets?

    a. Library reference.

    b. Training & mentoring.

    c. PM Services.

    d. All of the above.

15. The PMO function – 'Provide an independent view to the senior management' falls into which of the 4 baskets?

    a. Library reference.

    b. Training & mentoring.

    c. PM Services.

    d. Strategic Support.

16. The PMO function – 'Raise red flags' falls into which of the 4 baskets?

    a. Library reference.

    b. Training & mentoring.

    c. PM Services.

    d. Strategic Support.

17. The PMO function – 'Provide assistance to PM in developing/tracking project schedules' falls into which of the 4 baskets?

    a. Library reference.

    b. Training & mentoring.

    c. PM Services.

    d. Strategic Support.

18. The PMO function – 'Compile the project MIS' falls into which of the 4 baskets?

    a. Library reference.

    b. Training & mentoring.

    c. PM Services.

    d. Strategic Support.

19. The PMO function – 'Impart training to Project Managers' falls into which of the 4 baskets?

    a. Library reference.

    b. Training & mentoring.

    c. PM Services.

    d. Strategic Support.

For premium exclusive videos, visit https://vimeo.com/ondemand/pmowonderland or contact us at dg@dgonline.in for special discounted prices, quizzes, & 12 PDUs.

Chapter 09

Competency Assessment & Development!

We are learning the concepts and implementation aspects of project and program management office set up. We have travelled 8 chapters by now.

We have seen the wonder perspective, roaming buffalos, need for ambidexterity and we have also pulled 63 strings! We focused on the fundamental connection between project & program management with PMO in the earlier chapter. We saw one real life example of a senior leader demanding the PMO set-up for the name-sake.

We then listed the characteristics of the name-sake PMO. We also elaborated the 4 baskets of PMO. We also discussed all the functions of PMO, except one.

Let me welcome you to the 9th Chapter to elaborate the most important function of the PMO – Assessing & developing the project & program management competencies.

So – library reference, mentoring/training, PM services and Strategic representation are the four baskets of support that a PMO should focus on. That's what PMO is all about. One must see the contribution of PMO in competency development. How do these PMO services ultimately contribute in PM Competency Assessment and Development?

Assessment is definitely PMO's focus to understand the current competency battery in the organization. This falls under "Library Reference" category of the PMO services. This exercise gives the strong data on the state of the PM competencies of current and would be project & program managers. Let's see a real data for the competency assessment.

This is a real life example of PM Competency assessment of more than 300 project and program managers in a matured organizations..

I have developed a model of PM Competency Assessment & Development in 2005. Many organizations at present are using this. This assessment and development was done using my model.

The model is based on the fundamental belief that the "Person cannot be (should not be) graded. It is the competency of a person that should be graded." With this belief, we observe that a person appears in different grades. To be more correct, the project & program management competencies for a given person falls under various grades.

The competency assessment & development exercise must aim at bringing the best out of a project & program manager. The book elaborates the concept & practical approach with the help of real life case studies. The model uses more than 50 action-oriented definitions of PM Competencies.

The entire model with practical cases is explained in my book "Assessing & developing PM Competencies – A Case".

The competency spread in the organization is shown in the figure. The figure represents the grades of the PM Competencies. We get to know that there is 2.38 % + 18.10% + 49.05% = 69.52% rounded to 70% competency population is found in Grade 1, 2, and 3 zone. And 26.19%+4.29% = 30.48% rounded to 30% of competency population is found in Grade 4 and 5 zone.

1	2	3	4	5
		69.52	26.19 + 4.29 = 30.48	

- Vocabulary. Awareness Training
- Handholding. Facilitation Support.
- Mentoring by capable people external & internal
- New concept build-up. Tailoring Support

| Ignorance | | Attitude | Vision |

Practice & Participation

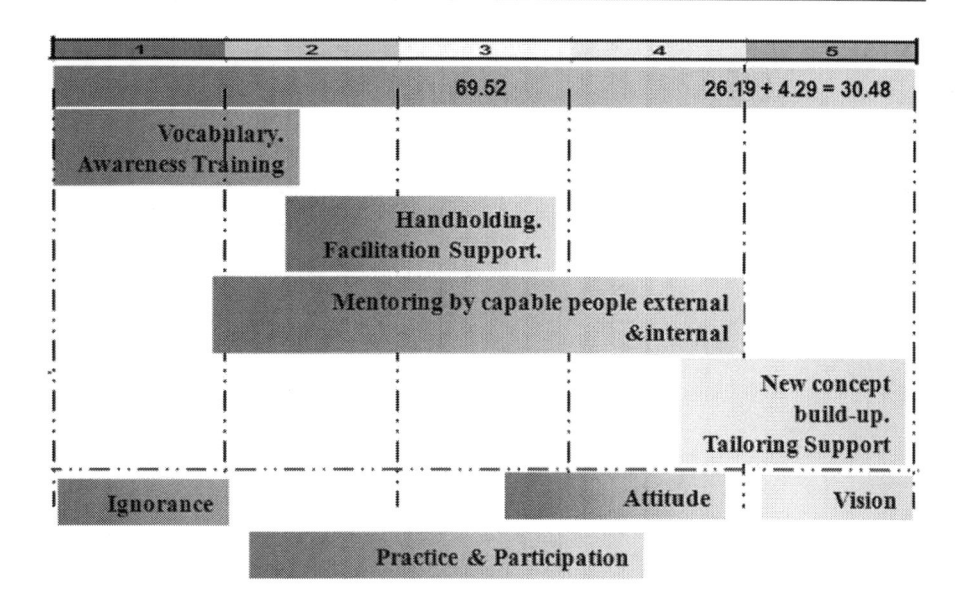

It is the set of people with competencies appearing in Grade 4 and 5 zone, can transform competencies appearing in the grades 1, 2, and 3 to grades at 4 and 5 level.

We need wisdom in the organization that is represented by Grade 4 and 5. That is actually PMO's job.

The four main issues are – Ignorance, Impediments in practice & participation, attitudinal problems, and Lack of food for thought/Vision. These issues are connected to Competency Grades.

Grade 1 is influenced by Ignorance.

Grade 2 & 3 is influenced by Impediments in Practice & Participation.

Grade 4 is influenced by Attitudinal Problems.

Grade 5 is influenced by need for food for thought.

The solutions to these are distinctly different.

For Grade 1 that is influenced by Ignorance, we need to provide Awareness build up trainings.

Grade 2 & 3 that is influenced by Impediments in Practice & Participation, we need to provide Handholding, on the job support, mentoring by internal and external experts.

Grade 4 that is influenced by Attitudinal Problems, we need to engage and motivate them to provide help to other in on the job support.

Grade 5 that is influenced by need for food for thought, we need to engage them in new concept building, research work, methodology refinements programs. This is the grade where we can look for developing the mentors.

The competency assessment & development exercise must aim at bringing the best out of a project & program manager.
The book elaborates the concept & practical approach with the help of real life case studies. The model uses more than 50 action-oriented definitions of PM Competencies.

This is the contribution of the PMO in developing the project & program management competencies.

Before moving to the next chapter, let's take a small quiz.

Mark the Statements True or False

1. First step to develop PM competency is to assess the current competency levels across organizations.

2. People can be graded as per the assessment.

3. DG has developed a model of competency assessment based on the belief that 'A person should not be graded. The competency in the person should be graded'.

4. A person can have all the competencies graded at 5th grade.

5. The person having more than 80% competencies graded at 5th Grade does not need additional support and development.

6. Knowledge, Skill, and Attitude are the 3 components of a concept of competency!

Select the One Right Option from a, b, c, d

7. Grade 1 in the model developed by DG, is influenced by which of the following parameter?

    a. Ignorance.

    b. Impediments in practice.

    c. Attitudinal problems.

    d. Lack of food for thought.

8. Grade 2 in the model developed by DG, is influenced by which of the following parameter?

    a. Ignorance.

    b. Impediments in practice.

    c. Attitudinal problems.

    d. Lack of food for thought.

9. Grade 3 in the model developed by DG, is influenced by which of the following parameter?

    a. Ignorance.

    b. Impediments in practice.

    c. Attitudinal problems.

    d. Lack of food for thought.

10. Grade 4 in the model developed by DG, is influenced by which of the following parameter?

    a. Ignorance.

    b. Impediments in practice.

    c. Attitudinal problems.

    d. Lack of food for thought.

11. Grade 5 in the model developed by DG, is influenced by which of the following parameter?

    a. Ignorance.

    b. Impediments in practice.

    c. Attitudinal problems.

    d. Lack of food for thought.

12. DG proposes which of the following strategy to counter the issues faced at Grade 1 in the PM competency assessment & development model developed by DG?

    a. Mentoring.

    b. Awareness & interest build-up trainings.

    c. New concept building engagement.

    d. On the job support.

13. DG proposes which of the following strategy to counter the issues faced at Grade 2 in the PM competency assessment & development model developed by DG?

    a. Mentoring.

    b. Awareness & interest build-up trainings.

    c. New concept building engagement.

    d. On the job support.

14. DG proposes which of the following strategy to counter the issues faced at Grade 3 in the PM competency assessment & development model developed by DG?

    a. Mentoring.

    b. Awareness & interest build-up trainings.

    c. New concept building engagement.

    d. On the job support.

15. DG proposes which of the following strategy to counter the issues faced at Grade 5 in the PM competency assessment & development model developed by DG?

    a. Mentoring.

    b. Awareness & interest build-up trainings.

    c. New concept building engagement.

    d. On the job support.

For premium exclusive videos, visit https://vimeo.com/ondemand/pmowonderland or contact us at dg@dgonline.in for special discounted prices, quizzes, & 12 PDUs.

Chapter 10

PM Competency Assessment

We are learning the concepts and implementation aspects of project and program management office set up. We have travelled 9 chapters by now. We have seen the wonder perspective, roaming buffalos, need for ambidexterity and we have also pulled 63 strings! We focused on the fundamental connection between project & program management with PMO in the earlier chapter.

We saw one real life example of a senior leader demanding the PMO set-up for the name-sake. We then listed the characteristics of the name-sake PMO. We also elaborated the 4 baskets of PMO.

We also discussed all the functions of PMO, except one. We also enlisted the issues at different competency grades and solutions to those. We elaborated the most important role of the PMO – Competency Development!

Let me welcome you to the 10th Chapter. It is a most elaborated chapter of the book. Now in this chapter let's have a deep dive in the subject of competency assessment & development. The competency assessment & development exercise must aim at bringing the best out of a project & program manager.

> *The competency assessment & development exercise must aim at bringing the best out of a project & program manager.*

It elaborates the concept & practical approach with the help of real life case studies. The model uses more than 50 action-oriented definitions of PM Competencies. It presents the practicalities involved in assessing & developing the PM competencies.

> *"A person is NEVER graded.*
> *The competencies of a person are graded.*
> *So a person is present in all Grades exhibiting competencies in different grades."*

"One who understands this subtlety can reap the benefit of competency assessment in terms of individual and hence organizational growth."

– Dhananjay Gokhale

A number of organizations try to define and document project manager competencies. Many factors like a sound understanding of competencies, competency grades, facilitators' interviewing & inference skills, etc. play a very important role in such an exercise. The exercise must aim at bringing the best out of a project manager with honest efforts to help the PM successfully continuing the journey towards excellence! The key is to go beyond mere processes and create a mapping exercise based on action-oriented competency statements.

This chapter not only elaborates the concept, but it actually puts forward the 'How to' aspects with the help of a real-life case study of a project management competency mapping exercise based on more than 50 action-oriented definitions of PM Competencies.

10.1 The Objective of the Project Manager

Please answer the following question before you continue reading –

"What is the objective of the project manager?"

If you want to ENJOY...

then please write your answer in this text box before you read further.

If you need more space, then use the back side of this page.

I have always asked this question since 2001 at the beginning of each session that I've conducted in the project management domain. Surprisingly, every time the audience missed the point. Each time I got the answer for the question that I never asked.

The set of answers that I got since 2001 are...

- *"to satisfy the stakeholder"*
- *"to manage resources"*
- *"to complete the project within time and budget and as per the quality requirements"*
- *"to complete the project successfully"*
- *"to manage the risks in the project"*

And so many…

So, what is your answer? ☺ ☺

Something similar to the one above?

Be alert, the question is…

"What is the objective of the project manager?"

The above answers may appear correct as per the theory books. These answers may help pleasing the boss. The answers are politically correct and socially accepted. But none of them really hits the nail answering the true objective of the project manager.

If you see the set of answers that people generally express, all of them mainly echo the 'actions' or 'responsibilities' of the project manager. The above answers are more suitable for the question – 'What does a project manager do?' or 'What are the responsibilities of the project manager?' or 'What are the functions of project management?' However, none of the answers defines the objective of the project manager.

Let's do one experiment.

Let's ask a question 'What if, I as a PM do not…' to each on the answers and try answering them.

- What if I do not satisfy the stakeholders?
- What if I do not complete the project within time, budget and as per quality requirements?
- What if I do not complete the project successfully?
- What is I do not manage the risks in the project?

Or, let's ask a question 'why?' to each one of the answers and try answering the same.

- **Why** *"to satisfy the stakeholders"?*
- **Why** *"to manage resources"?*
- **Why** *"to complete the project within time and budget and as per the quality requirements"?*
- **Why** *"to complete the project successfully"?*
- **Why** *"to manage the risks in the project"?*

In either way, if a person really ponders honestly, the inner voice responds. The objective is **Moksha** ☺.

The objective of the project manager is...

To get out OR come out of the project.

10.2 Context of PM Competency

"The objective of the project manager is to get out or come out of the project".

Invariably in past 16 years I have heard silence after I state this!

☺ ☺...*Is this objective difficult to digest?*

I have seen lots of project managers in last 16 years hesitate to accept this as an objective. They have been hammered with a thought that the objective of a PM is to satisfy the customer OR to complete the project on time within the budget.

If one asks a simple question 'why?' to all these so called objectives, the ultimate truth comes out as "I, as a project manager want to come out of the project **successfully or happily** ☺" By now the participants with whom I dwell upon this further are comfortable especially when I add two words – happily or successfully.

What does one mean by "successfully or happily coming out of project?" It is all about taking care of basic instinct of a human being. **Curiosity** is one of the basic instincts of human being.

Project is all about managing stakeholders. Each of the stakeholders in the project is fundamentally a human being. And every individual, unless a self-realized soul, wants to know about future. Project manager needs to satisfy this drive of the stakeholders. Project Management success is all about bringing this awareness. The project management can be successful when the facts related to current and future progress of the project are maintained and communicated quantitatively in a continuous real-time manner.

So the objective can be further elaborated as —

The objective of PM is –

"To come out or get out of the project by bringing in quantitative Visibility & Predictability throughout the project in real time manner in an ever changing project environment".

This fundamental clarity would make the further reading more contributory. The competency of a project manager can be mapped fundamentally on the clarity of this concept. The project management science then can assist in making person understand the best practices, theory, tools, and techniques.

Project Management competency assessment is a very first step in developing competency through intrinsic willingness of the project managers. However unless one implements the learning, the competency cannot be developed. And the implementation should be through 'intrinsic willingness' and not for external governance.

Project Management competency assessment is a very first step in developing competency through intrinsic willingness of the project managers.

The book explains the model based on a real life experiences.

10.3 Need of PM Competency Assessment

Echoing through the corridors of our organization we often hear these refrains:

- We plan to hire a new project manager…how can we predict which candidate will perform best?
- We want to give project management training to some of our junior team members…how can we be sure which ones are the most likely to succeed at project management?
- We are reviewing proposals from several vendors for a project that is critical to our company's future…how can we assess if the vendor project manager is competent?
- We are growing in size and are expecting a new large fixed price projects. Our client is extremely focused on project managers' competency. Who can we select to be the project manager for this project?

And this is not limited to chat around the coffee machine alone. These are even heard in the board rooms, conference rooms, all-hands meets, canteens, cabs, and across many interactions.

These are the concerns that engage senior management as well; and find an echo in the words of the CEO who declares,

"Our organization is growing by leaps and bounds in all aspects such as manpower, clients, revenue, locations, certifications, and benchmarking! We need to prepare our middle management for executing and managing large, fix-bid projects."

The concern indeed is genuine. And the answer does not lay in the past performance alone. The key action is to implement a pool of competent project managers. It is necessary then to mentor the project managers while improving their PM competencies.

One needs to be really confident in the abilities of the project managers. Therefore there exists a need of objectively & reliably assessing the abilities. The development is possible only when one understands the current status of abilities.

It is imperative to understand the activities that a project manager does. It is worth answering a seemingly simple question – "What does a PM do?"

10.4 Project Management – a 3D Model!

I am a mechanical engineer by education. Like most of the mechanical engineers, I too do not understand any things scripted in any language other than pictures and models. The following diagram explains the way I have understood the project management.

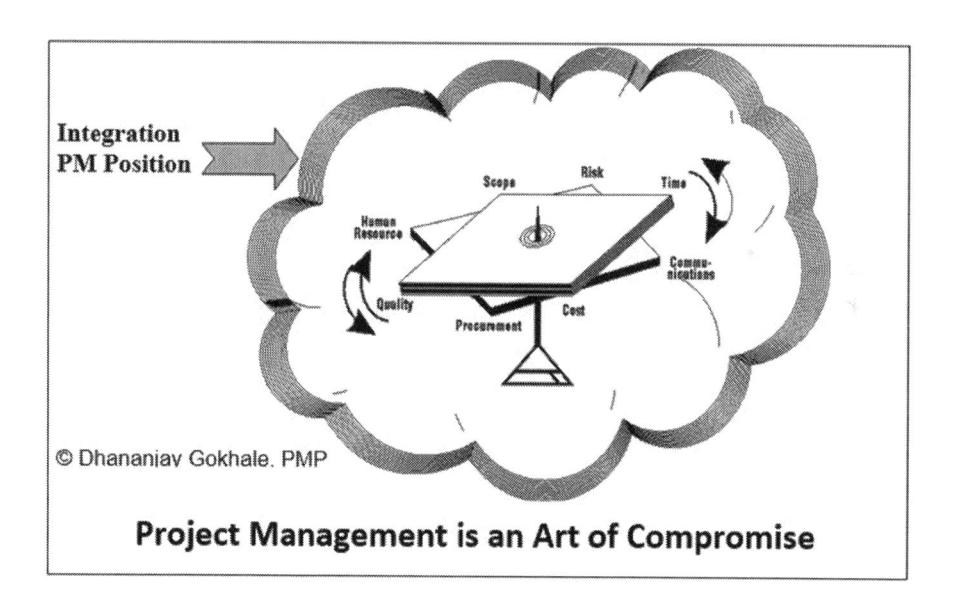

Project Management is an Art of Compromise

Let's say a project has milestone planned at two weeks from now. Having done some analysis, it was understood that the milestone would get delayed by one week. What all actions that a project team can take at this juncture of the project?

Some suggest increasing the resources, while some suggest communicating and getting approval for the delay from the client. Some others consider reducing the features, while some suggest getting help from vendors.

Now, if I have to explain it with the help of the model then it goes like this. When the milestone is getting delayed, it can be represented as Time vertex of the plane, leaving its position, goes down. The plane has lost its horizontal equilibrium. The intention behind every suggestion we got, was to gain back the original horizontal equilibrium. It can happen by either pushing or pulling the vertices in the model.

In short, at any point of time, PM has to maintain, at least, the plane of Scope –Time – Cost – Quality horizontal!

And most important aspect is while doing so PM should not stand on the plane but should be out and above, to have an entire integrated view of the total project.

So PM's position is at Integration.

Therfore, the key responsibility of the PM is to maintain the planes in horizontal equilibrium. Now, let's see how one can systematically think and work on it.

10.5 7 Verbs and 9 Nouns of Project Management

We have seen these strings earlier. Let's revise.!

The horizontal equilibrium is achieved by applying either pull or push forces on the vertices of the plane. Now, it's a game of Verbs and Nouns. Verbs are the forces known as project management "Process Groups" while nouns are the vertices known as project management "Knowledge Areas".

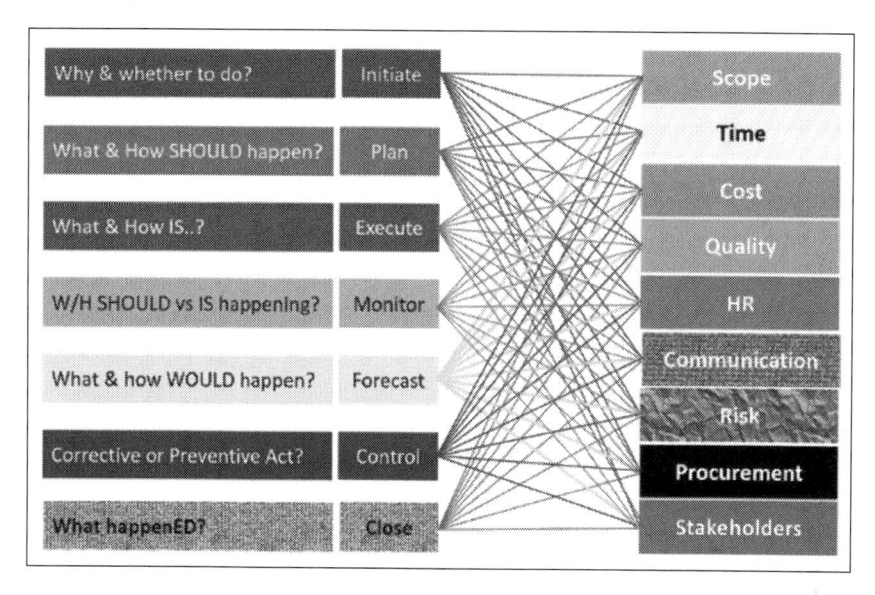

Why & whether to do?	Initiate		Scope
What & How SHOULD happen?	Plan		Time
			Cost
What & How IS..?	Execute		Quality
W/H SHOULD vs IS happening?	Monitor		HR
			Communication
What & how WOULD happen?	Forecast		Risk
Corrective or Preventive Act?	Control		Procurement
What happenED?	Close		Stakeholders

A project manager has 7 verbs at her disposal. They are – initiate, plan, execute, monitor, forecast, control, & close. Each verb has its own mindset. It is better explained by the corresponding questions as indicated in the Exhibit 2. A project manager constantly should ask and seek quantitative answers for the 7 simple questions.

Each question needs to be asked in the context of each noun. There shall therefore be 63 combinations possible of these 7 verbs and 9 nouns. Those are the threads shown in the Exhibit 2 above. **Each thread represents and action.** The thread is conjunction of Verb <-> Noun.

E.g. assume, that I am managing a small (?☺) & simple (?☺) project of Passing PMP® Examination. I am a project manager and should seek the quantitative answers for a question – "What is happening?" on each area. Following is an example of questions and answers!

So, **what is happening on...**

Scope?	PMI Membership is sought. 35 Contact Hours workshop is 50% done. In self-study, 3 processes are understood thoroughly. 25 questions are solved as a practice.
Time?	7 days are over.
Cost?	INR 15000/– paid.
Quality?	Facilitation specifications are achieved. My self-study quality in terms of focus on the subject matter is 7 on the scale of 10. Mock questions – first set of 10 questions were not ok as they were not at par with PMI standards. Later 25 were perfect.
HR?	Two people are not performing as per the responsibilities. Rest all are ok on their work.
Communication?	2 issues on communication reported. Rest communications are taking place.
Risk?	7 Risks are identified. Response actions are being taken on 3 prioritized risks.
Procurement?	2 SOWs sent. 1 contract finalized for transport for group study. Could not start drafting of the 4th SOW.
Stakeholders?	2 stakeholders added. 1 moved.

The above table is a sample example. It is mainly to elaborate how each question needs to be answered in all 9 contexts. So now one can more systematically understand the responsibilities or actions that a competent project manager should do. There shall be sixty three of them.

Now look at this broader and comprehensive perspective in the following manner...

1. The objective of the project manager is get out of the project successfully or happily.

2. Successfully or happily means bringing in quantitative visibility and predictability in the project throughout.

3. This quantitative visibility and predictability contributes in satisfying the curiosity of the project stakeholders increasing the chances of gaining active support from the stakeholders.

4. This further helps in taking apt corrective and preventive actions keeping project on track increasing the chances of happy☺ release of the project manager.

5. And to make it happen the project manager should take sixty three actions.

The underlying truth is that the Project Manager is constantly trying to balance the two planes with a game of puling and/or pushing the vertices. The competent project manager does it very smooth and calculated steps. Whereas others end up with fire-fighting. The entire competency assessment exercise is based on the game of 7 verbs and 9 nouns. Hence one must understand the above concept to get a comprehensive understanding of the competency mapping exercise.

I feel Project Management is all about pulling strings ☺.

10.6 What Is Competency?

Dictionary definitions often fall short in describing a concept. But the leading companies might describe a Competency as "a cluster of related knowledge, skills, and attitudes that…

- Affects a major part of one's job.
- Correlates with performance on the job.
- Can be measured against well-accepted standards.
- Can be improved via training and development".

(Source: Scott Parry 1998, Project Management Competency Development Framework, PMI).

A competency is what a successful employee must be able to do to accomplish desired results on a job.

Competencies are built up over time and are not innate. It typically takes experience on the job to build competencies. Knowledge, Skills and Abilities (KSAs), by contrast, might be brought into the job by entry-level employees. For example, an entry-level accountant who has just completed college might know the Income Tax Code and basic accounting principles. Yet it is unlikely that this person would be competent at filing a corporate tax return. This is another way of saying that the employee has the KSAs that underlie the job but has not yet developed the job competencies. Development and experience are needed to become competent.

> *Knowledge, Skills and Attitude is a tripod of competency.*

Arjuna asks four questions about the competencies. They are indeed wonderful, succinct yet comprehensive. They give us the four aspects of competencies. If we use these 4 questions, then the definition of the competencies will be very apt. The four questions are.

का भाषा? [Ka (what) Bhasha (description)]

    What is he like? What is his nature?

किम् प्रभाषेत? [Kim (how) Prabhashet (speak/conduct)]

    How does he express himself through conduct of life?

किम् आसीत? [Kim (now) Aaseet (sit)]

    How is the inner nature? What happens within him?

व्रजेत किम्? [Vrajet (act/respond) Kim (how)]

    How does he respond to the world?

So while defining any competency, we should answer the above 4 questions.

For example, let's try to answer these questions in the context of an individual who is competent of Identify Risk process.

What is he like? What is his nature?

Observant, alert, quite open, happy go lucky, does not get tensed, and, sees far future.

How does he express himself through conduct of life?

Does not really need anybody's permission to speak, jells well with others,

Keeps himself aware about new categories of risks.

Communicates uncertainties clearly without creating biases.

How's the competent person's inner nature?

Calm, Egoless, does not feel insulted.

Quite open about positive things around.

How's the competent person's response to the world?

Lists the uncertainties objectively and help others in that.

Welcomes the new information very openly.

Does not label the person or situation.

10.7 Constituents of PM Competency

Project Management competency has three constituents.

- Project Management Knowledge i.e. what an individual knows about Project Management,

- Project Management Performance i.e. what an individual is able to do while applying Project Management knowledge, and

- Personal Competency i.e. how an individual behaves while performing on project(s).

(Source: Project Management Competency Development Framework, PMI)

Examples of Project Management Competency

Project Scope Management Competency

These are the competencies that a PM engaged in Project Scope Management must have:

- Develops and maintains the processes for linking and co-ordination of project control mechanisms.

- Depicts the relationship between scope, performance, time, cost, and quality in terms of thresholds settings.

- Able to show/present the pictorial view of the project scope using WBS and other suitable mechanisms.

- States clearly the interfaces arising because of exclusion.

- Creates common understanding about the inclusion, exclusion, and grouping of scope items.

- Enlists clearly the probable sources of changes and sets mechanisms in advance.

Project Initiation Competencies

These are the competencies that a PM engaged in Project Initiation must have:

- Uses (exploits) the Project Charter (PC) as an effective tool to set the ground for further planning and controlling exercise.

- Insists on a project charter and getting it acknowledged/ understood by.

- Makes the 'Initiating' perceptible for each phase of the project by formally delegating/announcing the phase.

- Identifies the project stakeholders (However trivial anyone of them may sound!).

- Understands the constraints/assumptions/objectives as seen by the client site project manager.

- Understands the client's maturity/capabilities in various areas.

- Identifies/understands the type/complexity/size of the project; risk tolerance levels; and quality objectives.

- Visualizes the project's overall solution/basic strategy/critical success factors.

Personal Competency

Conflict management competencies

A crucial part of a project manager's competencies is the ability to manage conflicts within and around the project.

A PM must:

- Be able to express opinions directly and clearly without abuse.
- Listen to the opinions and feelings of others and demonstrates understanding by restatement.
- Communicate disagreement to stakeholders as necessary.
- Ask for negative feedback in order to learn.

(Source: 'Building Robust Competencies', by Paul C Green).

10.8 Grades of Project Management Competency

In the ancient Indian Vedic scriptures like Shree Bhagwad Geeta three pathways of attaining realization are described. They are DnyanYoga, KarmaYoga, and BhaktiYoga. I love to connect three integral parts of competency – Knowledge, Skill, and Attitude to these three yogas. The scholars may apprehend this statement. However I am connecting it at a very high level. They are not silos but are heavily integrated.

An individual for a specific competency can be found in any of the row below.

Expression for a given competency	Knowledge Dnyan Yog	Skill Karma Yog	Attitude Bhakti Yog
I do not know & don't want to know	Absent	Absent	Absent
I do not know & eager to know	Absent	Absent	Present
I know but I can't & don't want to do	Present	Absent	Absent
I know but I can't do but eager to do	Present	Absent	Present
I know, I am doing to some extent & I am ok with what I am doing	Present	Present	Absent
I know, I am doing to some extent and eager to get support	Present	Present	Present
I know, I can do it well, but I don't feel like doing it.	Present	Present	Absent
I know, I can, I am doing it well, and I can motivate others while improving self	Present	Present	Present

Not Aware about needs lot of improvement	Aware but don't know how to do it	Aware, partial & unconfident implementation	Aware confident implementation, though focus is compliance for sake	Confident, proactive adaptable implementation, can mentor
1	2	3	4	5

REMEMBER: *It is not the person but the competencies of a person that are graded.*

So a person is present in all grades exhibiting competencies in different grades.

I proposed that project management competencies can be graded on the following scale:

Grade 1: Lack of awareness

Participants exhibiting competencies graded at this grade are found to be ignorant of the purpose and importance of that particular competency.

<u>Example:</u> When asked to list the contents and importance of the monthly Project Status Report (PSR) the typical response is, "Actually I don't get time to fill PSR in detail. Somebody from the team completes the formality."

Grade 2: Aware but partial and unconfident implementation

Participants exhibiting competencies graded at this grade exhibit awareness of the purpose and importance of project management processes and knowledge areas. However, there is very little implementation of the knowledge.

<u>Example:</u> When faced with the same question as above, the answer offered here is, "It consumes lot of time and number of things are needed to be captured and calculated, hence we manage to get it filled by a team member. Mostly copy-paste and revise is the practice."

Grade 3: Aware of Project Management and Organizational Processes but unconfident implementation

Participants exhibiting competencies graded at this grade exhibit an awareness of the purpose and importance of the project management processes & knowledge areas. On matters of implementation, the minimum level of conformance is achieved. However, the project manager is not sold on to the relevance of the entire exercise. Its impact on the actual day-to-day running of the project is not apparent to the person and thus implementation is viewed more as a compulsory chore rather than an aid to one's efforts.

Example: Here the answer to the PSR query is likely to be, "We submit the PSR every month. But nobody fills time sheets honestly hence it is difficult to capture metrics inputs. And hence the formalities are completed but they are of no use."

Grade 4: Knowledge of Project Management and Organizational Processes and confident implementation

A Project Manager exhibiting competencies graded at this grade exhibits the knowledge of the purpose and importance of the project management processes & knowledge areas. In implementation, the project manager achieves the maximum level of conformance. Moreover there is full awareness of the relevance of the processes engaged in.

Example: Such a person's answer to the PSR query will be, "We submit the PSR every month. Although it takes some time, we need to fill it. Calculating the number of metrics manually for this report is the main pain area. We try to get the information from team members and generate data for the PSR. Although Metrics generation and getting productivity figures is based on this report, it has not been given the importance it deserves because nobody reviews it."

Grade 5: Knowledge of PM & Org. processes and proactive implementation

A Project Manager exhibiting competencies graded at this grade exhibits complete knowledge of the purpose and importance of project management processes & knowledge areas. There is a demonstrably clear awareness of the crux of the matter. Not only does this individual's implementation fully conform to the laid down norms, there is also a mindset of continuously improving.

Example: Such a project manager is of the opinion that, "A PSR is a monthly project report. It contains the Progress & Status of the project apart from generating the requisite metrics. Team members are encouraged to fill in true data so as to capture real figures for the metrics calculations. I have prepared an Excel sheet with certain formulae that takes care of few calculations. But we need to give a thought to which metrics are really applicable to what type of project so that unnecessary data is not collected resulting in saving the PM's Time and Efforts."

10.9 Background of the Case

A Project Management Competency Mapping exercise was conducted in a CMM level 5 organization having operations in India, the UK and the US and with employee strength of 1400. 30 employees were part of the study. All 30 of these were project directors, senior project managers, project managers, and project leaders.

Objective

The exercise aimed to get the evidence of the Project Managers' application of knowledge, their ability to give tangibility & bring in predictability to the project, and their compliance with the performance criteria for competency.

Methodology

The modus operandi of the study included:

- Interviews and personal interactions with the subjects.
- Evaluation of project managers and processes.
- Document checks.
- Assessing level of understanding and knowledge of PM concepts, use of tools/techniques/methodologies.
- Understanding pain areas.

- Making notes.

- Voice recording of discussions (with the individual's consent).

10.10 Why Interview? Why Not Any Other Method?

The most important part of the assessment is the interview that I conduct of the project managers. It is always interesting to know the person and the work.

I dwelled a lot on which type of instrument that I should be using while developing the model of competency assessment. Many suggested going for multiple choice objective questions – MCQs. It is a faster tool. It can assess one's knowledge to some extent. However when it comes to performance, the MCQ pattern does not help. Further if one decides, then one can crack the pattern of the questions.

Most important aspect is that the question paper or questionnaire – either open ended, close ended, or MCQs – does not create the bonding and openness necessary to get to know the person and the competencies.

The focus of the assessment is finding out the strengths in people. It is not to grade anyone. In such a case, the openness is the foundation. The trust created should generate the courage in participants enough to openly admit the weak competencies. It should also create courtesy to share the level of expertise in egoless manner. This is possible only when one creates the trust. The more opportunity lies in the personal face to face interaction than a paper based assessment.

10.11 What-If

...a participant do not share openly, especially when they know that it is for assessment?

There was a glimpse of a negative thought – 'what if the participant do not share the things openly?' OR 'what if the participant disguised the assessment?' This was indeed a scary thought, especially 11 years ago when this model was being developed. I had no proven records, neither any big institution backing my hypothesis when I proposed this model for very first time. The organization leader, who allowed me to make use of this model of assessing the competency, had nothing to support the decision. I owe him a lot in addition to appreciating his courage.

> ***Nevertheless, I had strong belief that this method will work.***

The first reason behind this confidence was my open motive. My intention was extremely pure. I wanted to find out the strengths in the person whom I will interview. And when the genuine intention is explained transparently, I have always seen people believing in & supporting it.

The second reason is that I trusted my intervention and interview skills. I always liked to listen to people, about their work, their ideas. Although it was always due to my inner drive to know more from the expert. I had lots of interactions done with many professionals in their work environment. Let it be a Chef or a Lobby Manager of a hotel, or Bus Conductor, or a Cartoonist, or an Air Traffic Controller, or a flight despatcher, or Bhelpuri Wala! ☺. So this was an experience that I could share with the CEO of the organization who allowed me to do assessment 11 years ago.

When your intentions are clear, your interest is genuine, then people share. I firmly believe that you get to know the strengths in people.

The third aspect that reinforced my belief is my little bit exposure of knowing and grasping personality types of the people. I had a hobby and even now I keep observing people, without getting indulged, of course. ☺ I had done MBTI (Myers Briggs Type Indicator) Accreditation from Australian Psychologist Press. This was purely out of my hobby. However this hobby and this formal education served a lot in strengthening the belief in the model.

My belief was necessary. However, it was imperative to bring in couple of more techniques to create a strong antidote for the failure mode of people not sharing openly. I always trusted on public exposure and public commitment. So in addition to above three aspects, I ensure following actions.

First, the entire methodology was explained in the kick-off meeting before the assessment. All the doubts of the participants were cleared.

Second, the entire exercise was 'de-linked' from the performance appraisal and incentive mechanism. The organization leader gave a written commitment that the data, if any, shall not be used in performance appraisal system. It was instead connected to mentor-mentee system.

Third, it was agreed upon and announced that no superior shall be present during the interviews of the subordinates.

Fourth, it was made extremely clear to all involved that this assessment is not of an individual. But it is to know the grades of competencies of an individual.

Today, having used this model for so many years, I can say that my belief, the reasons behind it and the basic 4 actions that I ensured have contributed totally to the success of this model. More importantly, the organizations have got the real assessment to build up their development models.

> *Hey, and did I tell you that I audio recorded each and every interview?* ☺

Of course with the knowledge and consent of each participant? It served as an amazing audio self-portrait on the PM Competency. Each individual was given back the audio recording and lots of them heard it over again. ☺

10.12 Interviews – Interesting & Intriguing

After having set up the expectations in the group meetings, having the leader of the organizations committing to the transparent & contributory use of the assessment, the interviews environment was somewhat open.

Of course, as a human nature, skepticism was seen during the very beginning of the interviews. Nevertheless the clear intentions and hence genuine focus has reached the audiences. It happens in all the assessments I have conducted so far. The only way forward is to start conversation with eye to eye connect.

The place of the interview was absolutely left to be chosen by the participants – meeting room, his or her desk, cafeteria, resting place, refreshing room, walk-ways, terraces, and any place where participant felt comfortable. Whenever participant used to choose the place other than the cabin or cubical, I felt I was happier than the participant. ☺. This took care of physical environment.

Emotional environment is second part which is extremely important to achieve. The environment should be conducive for participants to share their views transparently.

First thing that I used to do is quickly narrate my weaknesses in project management while explaining the overall experience that I have in this field. The narration of my weakness was absolutely genuine. I personally was honestly interested to know the way forward to improve up on those couple of competencies. I used to ask the participant about his or her idea that I could try to get over my weakness. Most of the cases this works.

The key point in any interview is breaking the ice and let the water flow. The above pattern of discussion gave me lot of emotional and physical ground to provide the candidate with this open foreground.

I say "I, many a time, get driven by the task oriented nature and that puts me on back seat in understanding the different personal perspectives about the person that I am interacting. Do you think that this is a problem with me? How can I get over it?' Then I quickly used to narrate my home construction project in the context of my weakness sharing how I damaged the relationship with my contractor once and what it took me to take it back on the similar resonance.

This helped participants in three ways.

First it gave them a wonderful platform to start sharing. Anyone is interested in guiding someone else, isn't it? ☺

Secondly, it reduced the fear and created willingness to share the failures.

And third, since I related the discussion to a personal project, away from the work, it created the need and interest to understand the perspective in holistic way. It subtly gave the hint that – 'application of principle are everywhere, seen in personal projects! It adds lot of value in retention and application of the theory."

Once this initial phase is handled well, the entire interview goes well. At times, I had to make the participant aware about the time limit of 90 minutes. ☺. Participants ended up sharing a lot of things and very openly.

Trust, is a very important factor. And I believe that at least 15 to 20% of the participants I interviewed knew since much before. They have seen me performing the tasks, working on projects, handling tough behaviors on personal, professional & social front. Most importantly, therefore they had high levels of trust on my intentions and actions.

10.13 Tough Behaviors

Even having taken care so meticulously about physical and mental environment, the tough behaviors are always expected. So there were few. I have my own ways to handle them. Some of the tough behaviors and the way I handled them are…

Meditative silence: ☺ some participants took long (very long) time to open up. It was not intentional every time. For those who did not know me, the silence was mainly for judging & testing me. At one side, I knew that there is a short time of 90 minutes for each interview and I cannot afford to extend time much beyond 10 minutes as the another participant is lined up after the interview. Nevertheless, I patiently digested the silence. If the person is of introvert preference, I used to ask very small, closed ended questions those actually were away from the introvert's definition of close to self. ☺. I used to share about my experience in equally short, crisp sentences, where I especially focus on systematically explaining (quickly) my intentions, reason the one should believe in me and the assessment. The best action after this that worked for me is a question that used to very smoothly flow from my side – 'where do you think the value can be added here?'

While bringing up this forte, I used to draw some schematic drawings on paper those are connected to project management. I used to draw it in a manner that it never appeared obvious but the same time the other side ended up getting intrigued in it expressing few words. And those few words are more than sufficient to pull of the gears. ☺ However, no matter what, I never touched my hand phone even in instances of unaware mind. ☺

My MBTI knowledge, practice, experience and exposure to lots of interactions earlier helped a lot in defining the pattern, content and right time for the questions. I have explained about it in next topic.

Maestro is here, salute! Some participants exhibited 'I know it all' behavior. The way I handled it is 'to salute'☺. These types of people are the best entertainers if you know how to get entertained. This maintains your energy level. This entertainment also helps your responses go in a manner that helps the other side to start sharing in more genuine manner.

The favorite lead lines of such participants are...

'These are not the ways the projects should be run...'

'In my last organization...'

'So, how are the competency levels of the people here?'

'Actually... (while speaking this single word is like – there is any person who knows it all, that person is no one else but almighty me☺)...'

'See, I will tell you...'

The moment I used to hear such lines anywhere in the interview, then immediately I used to salute. Of course, not in physical manner. The salute was in a form of expressions like 'Yes in fact, I wanted to hear it from you.' I don't think it is flattering, is it? No. These are the ways you develop unidirectional communication.

I had two challenges when I confront such participants. One is to validate their real depth or competencies. As many times there are people who have been trained as to how to look assertive, or how to face interviews more (?☺) confidently. Of course, it takes hardly a question or two to understand this.

Second possibility could be that the participant is really an expert. There is really lot to know from that person. There is a strong possibility that this person can be a good mentor and can be a good asset to the organization as his or her competencies on many areas are really well developed. Then why such an attitude has been built in? The challenge here is to make the person speak on the competencies. The challenge is to slow down, reduce and then eliminate the expressions of negative energies.

Who you? This was fantastic mesmerizing behavior. For a few seconds in the beginning of the intervention, I used to continuously remind myself – 'dear DG, you are interviewing him, be alert. ☺'. For, some participants used to take charge of the entire event so smoothly (I never felt bluntly☺)!

The wonderful lead lines of such participants are..

'Where have you done this exercise earlier?'

'Sometimes I wonder, how one can know the competencies in 90 minutes of interaction'

A story where a sage go on asking the king 'who are you?' ☺ is always remembered here. Such questions are obviously genuine irrespective of the lingual tone☺.

Even I had faced such questions in the very first assessment. I never had any issues answering such questions. Neither then, nor now! Once again the clear intentions that I had and my ability to express it equally clearly helped me.

I still remember my answer that I had given first time in the year 2004–05 to the questions – 'where have you done this exercise earlier?'

> *My answer was – 'This is my first formal exercise. The exercise is all about knowing and learning more about the wisdom in project management. The focus is all about finding strengths in the people. I have managed and also have supported projects in different industries. I have seen failures and success. And I am always eager to know the different perspectives to the situations that I have gone through. I firmly believe that the situations that I have gone through are NOT unique and hence are applicable to everyone and therefore I am here to interact with you'.*

It was then easy to answer this question as the number of assessments went on increasing. However, even today, the answer remains same except the first sentence.

10.14 Use of My Experiences in Psychological Types

I had a hobby and even now I keep observing people, without getting indulged, of course. ☺ I had done MBTI (Myers Briggs Type Indicator) Accreditation from Australian Psychologist Press. This was purely out of my hobby. However this hobby and this formal education served a lot in strengthening the belief in the model. The key success factors of the assessment model are openness & comprehensiveness in sharing done by the interview. This is all about sharing and communication.

Each one of us has own natural preferences in various aspects. The MBTI model that I studied and later got accredited practitioner in studies mainly preferences on 4 areas.

They are, **the way an individual...**

a. Directs the focus of attention & energy – Introversion & Extraversion.

b. Seeks the information from the world – Sensing & iNtuiating.

c. Responds & takes the decision, and – Thinking & Feeling.

d. Orients oneself to the outer world – Judging & Perceiving.

Each individual has one preference over other in each of the above pairs above. The interactions and communication patterns and behavior are influenced by these preferences. I was aware about these influences. Since I am practicing MBTI psychological type applications since 2005, it becomes easy to narrow down on the closest preferences of an individual during the interactions within the first few minutes. Once I used to get a feel of the preferences of a person in front; I tried to accommodate my way of interactions to suit the other side.

The awareness of these preference and hence using techniques to accommodate them largely creates preferential, conducive environment. I also observed that this also helps in reducing tough behaviors to a large extent. Even if a participant comes up with a skeptical or non-cooperative mindset; the conducive environment created in such a manner diminishes the resistance. And in a short period, the participant really starts responding extremely well.

Remember that using preference conducive techniques are no substitute for (a) the genuine interest in listening & learning, (b) transparency with sharer, (c) respect to the sharer. These three are the basics of foundation without which this entire exercise is futile.

Following are some sample examples that illustrates the way I used personality preferences to create the conducive environment during the interactions. I have explained it on the context of communications.

10.15 In Communications...

Introverts are more likely to (a) Keep things to themselves (b) Be calm and reserved & (c) Want autonomy. Therefore, while interacting with an 'Introverted' preference, it is advisable not to expect quick sharing. Not to push hard. It is necessary to create sumptuous space for that person without any disturbance. With such a personality I always get a page filled up before starting the verbal interactions. I give a page to read and check whether they have any expressions about it. This silence filled with reading/writing actions creates a space for an introvert. Once the interactions starts, I always appreciate the pauses that an introvert takes before the start of the speech. Most importantly, once an introvert starts speaking, I always wait till the answer is complete and then with a good pause, I put another question. ☺

Extraverts are more likely to (a) Share things openly, (b) Be enthusiastic and actively oriented, and (c) Want fellowship. Therefore, with such a preference I start with handshake, preferably standing close to the person. What helps is a few quick questions and sharing my mental or physical environment with that person with genuine urge to know about the interviewee. This is more than enough energy for a sharing to start. During the interactions, I always share my ideas even during halfway through the answers. Many times I even preferred asking the person to chat while walking towards a coffee vending machine or in the corridor.

Sensing types are more likely to (a) Enjoy practical conversations, (b) Move from point to point in liner fashion, (c) Use detailed description, and (d) Enhance messages using real and tangible experiences. Therefore, I always offer the description of the practical immediate use of this entire exercise during first 4 to 5 minutes of the interactions. And then I explain the entire process in step by step fashion. I generally avoid using far-fetched ideas, metaphors during interactions. The most important aspect is that I cite practical examples from my own personal life about advantages & disadvantages I had of using and not having the competencies.

iNtuitive types are more likely to (a) Enjoy clear conversations, (b) Skip around as they make connections, (c) Use metaphorical discussion, and (d) Enhance messages using imagination & ingenuity. Therefore, the impact of the exercise on a PM community as a whole and for the organization in coming years, are two points that I always describe. I love to listen to the ideas and utility of this exercise from this preference type. Most important thing that I never ever asked them to answer one by one. On the contrary, I listen to them as a story teller and then I draw inferences and present it to them which helps me in keeping myself on track☺ ☺, not them!

Thinking types are more likely to (a) Exhibit skepticism, (b) Be business-like, and (c) Start with critique or challenge. "Do you really think that one gets to know the competencies just by speaking with someone for 90 to 100 minutes?" Wow – Thinking type doubly confirmed! ☺ And, that always gives me a wonderful opportunity to quickly explain the 'objectivity' involved in the complete design. And this discussion itself brings in the environment that this type is looking for☺.

Feeling types are more likely to (a) Exhibit caring, (b) Be sociable, and (c) Start with praise. Therefore, I always ensure to seek and narrate the value that this type can add to the entire PM community and especially to someone who is trying to grow by sharing their experiences. "Have you sought any help from someone on any of the areas? How was the support? What did you like in that person?" – These are some opening patterns of the questions. This helps a lot. And then it becomes very easy to ask – "where can you help others? What is that area in project management that you can definitely add value to the PM community? Any recent experience where you really felt happy and deeply satisfied?" After this there comes a wonderful sharing of experiences helping me understanding & assessing the competencies.

Judging types are more likely to (a) Use decisive words – concluded, decided, (b) Orient discussions towards results/conclusions and expect summarization, and (c) Have a strong sense of time. "We will begin with overview discussion for 5 minutes, then you can share or ask your ideas or doubts. Would 5 minutes be fine? And then for 60 minutes we will chat on 6 areas on an average 10 minutes per area. I have kept 20 minutes buffer as the discussions become quite interesting sometimes." – ☺Trust me, this expression of schedule acts as a magic wand during the interactions with this type. A map and a clock are two necessary buddies in any journey ☺ ☺ for them!

Perceiving types are more likely to (a) Use hedging words – may be, perhaps, tend to, (b) Orient discussions towards options, and (c) Quite open with absence of schedule. Remember, not even 'S' of schedule☺. "We have roughly 1 – 1.5 hour. Let's chat for some time. I do not have any agenda as such, except few aspects about PM that I would like to know from you. Let's see how it goes."☺

Isn't there a 180˚ contrast in the expressions for above two types? Yes indeed! This is what I meant by creating a conducive environment. **WARNING:** Never ever express without genuine interest & respect. Else, you are sitting on a time bomb!

My own preferences combination is – **Introvert Sensing Thinking Judging.** So it was very easy when the interviewee also preferred the same preferences. I did not have to accommodate the behavior as it was also my natural preference set. As the similarity between my preferences and that of the interviewee's reduces; I need to become more and more alert. Imagine the situation when I conduct an in assessment interview of a person with preferences combination – **Extrovert iNtuitive Feeling Perceiving!** Of course, I need to be accommodative to all these completely opposite preferences. However this accommodation must be out of genuine interest in listening & learning and with heartfelt respect to the sharer. Else, I am the looser.

The stake involved is tremendous. The results of artificial behaviors could be catastrophic leading to absolutely unreliable competency assessment. And hence if one really wants to reap the benefits, the seeds of interactions must be treated with (a) the genuine interest in listening & learning, (b) transparency with sharer, (c) respect to the sharer. These three are the basics foundations without which this entire exercise is futile. And of course, the psychological understanding plays a vital role.

10.16 Parameters Defined for Assessments

I interact with the participants on the following areas of competencies. All these are interconnected.

1. Communication Matrix
2. Client Feedback
3. Project Records
4. Handholding contribution
5. Success Criteria – comparison
6. Project Diary
7. Project post-mortem
8. Informal info for closing
9. Contingencies & MR clarity
10. Team Cost Awareness
11. Cost Reduction alternatives
12. EV analysis
13. Cash in-out flow management
14. Project specific reward
15. Client side Org Structure
16. External feedback
17. Informal appraisal
18. Formal project-based appraisal
19. Sponsor education
20. Sponsor commitment
21. Project selection & roadmap
22. Project description
23. PMT establishment
24. Formal Initiation
25. PM's early involvement
26. Only required metrics
27. Causes & Lessons Learnt
28. Experience sharing sessions
29. Vendor rewards
30. High Standards for vendors
31. Quality – Cost connections

32. Customer Tolerance limit
33. Complete – True data
34. Client interaction frequency
35. Risk concept clarity
36. Risk connect to Objectives
37. Residual Risk
38. Risk responses
39. Unidentified Risk: Closure
40. Tangible measureable progress
41. Changes Thresholds Limits
42. Rework & CR – difference
43. Correctness – completeness
44. Business Opportunities
45. Schedule revisit
46. Reserve Time
47. Hard & Soft dependencies
48. Assumption checks
49. Alternatives sensitization
50. Would-Be clarity

10.17 Covering the Parameters in the Interview

There is no specific sequence in which I interact with the participant on these parameters. My focus is always on the coverage and not on the sequence. As all these parameters are interconnected, I always need to make a choice for interlinking parameters. It all depends upon the parameter that gets picked up in the opening interactions. A point of opening evolves itself within first couple of minutes.

For example, a very informal question goes from my side – "hi, how is the day today?" If the participant responds – "It was very taxing. The issue has come up and we were tied up in it". I think this can be a wonderful opportunity to maneuver the discussion to (a) risk or (b) client handling. So, here I have a choice.

I can decide to respond in one of the following ways...

a. "Yeah, I know. So now this will get added into your Issue Register, right? Was this issue earlier a risk that got identified in the risk register?" OR.

b. "Oh, it is tricky, isn't it? Generally how do you and the customer communicate with each other on such matter? What improvement that you think you and/or customer should target?"

If I decide to go for option (a), then it is easy to cover up parameters 35, 36, 37, 38, 39, 42, 31 and so on ☺.

OR if I get to know that the participant has just attended a meeting with the team OR client, the opening question can be "How was the meeting, and what is one thing that you would not repeat in the next meeting?" At times, you need to have patience to listen to the pause after this question. However, I consider that as a pregnant pause ☺. Lot to expect after that.

Many times, I have simply asked a seemingly simple question "what is the status of your project?" The answers heard after this are very cautious ☺. I enjoy watching the body language of the participants while answering this question. Inevitably, I have heard **'adjectives'** (like good, fine, hmmm..in fix, fantastic, so far so good)☺. I am not against using adjectives. However they must be followed by quantitative statement. So to an adjective heard, I always ask "why not superlative of that adjective"? For example – if the answer is **"good"** then I ask **"why not better? And what stops you calling from 'excellent'?"** ☺ This helps me maneuvering to 6, 12, 33, 43 ☺.

I always felt that this is similar to writing a screen play of a drama, based on audience response ☺.

10.18 Data and Related Inferences

As and when the interactions take place, the data is consolidated in a predefined worksheet. I also request participants to rate the 50 competencies in 5 different grades.

DG rating To/Org	Self Rating	Absolute Difference	Parameter	Description of parameter	Bhaven J PMO	Self 0	Ab	Hari
64 58%	71 71%	13%	Assumption checks	Assumptions made during task duration/efforts estimations are clearly documented & regularly analysed for their trueness with team's understanding	Y 1	4	3	
38 35%	68 68%	33%	Alternative schedules / strategy sensitization	Alternative schedules prepared as contingency and what if analysis for surprise response readiness and also the key stakeholders are sensitized on this aspect with clear understanding	Y 1	3	2	
44 40%	63 63%	23%	C'gencies & MR clarity	Contingencies, buffers & management reserves are understood clearly while working with cost overruns, change management & risk responses	Y 1	4	3	
74 67%	62 62%	5%	Qlty - Cost connections	Quality inputs are considered for cost budgeting, alternative identifications, and reductions	Y 3	3	0	
79 72%	63 63%	9%	Cust Tolerence limit	Customer tolerance limits hence internal control limits quantified for the product/service in simple manner	Y 4	3	1	
46 42%	61 61%	19%	Prj specific reward	Project specific rewards are planned in & explicitely explained and ensured that they are executed as decided	Y 1	2	1	
75 68%	75 75%	7%	Client side Org Structure	Client side organization structure is understood well	Y 3	3	0	

Org level inference   **Individual data**

This brings in individual data as shown on the right hand side of the Exhibit 1. There are mainly two columns. In the image you see one heading as 'Bhaven' consists rating by DG and other is 'Self' consists of self-rating. [Bhaven is a name of the participant project manager.] The adjacent column is the absolute difference between DG rating and Self-Rating. The acceptable difference threshold that I had coined was up to 2. When this number is 3 and above, it was considered as alert. The count of such discrepancy was accepted up to 5.

For example, as shown in the exhibit, there are two competencies where the absolute difference between DG and Self-Rating is equal to or more than 3. It is highlighted. Total such highlights should not be more than 5.

> *I was extremely happy when I see 96 to 97% cases matched and remained below absolute difference of 3. This is in fact the proof of validation of the interviewee's assessment closeness by me. The participants were also comfortable.*

The individual competency assessment data is ultimately used to understand the organization's competency. It is the individual that makes or breaks the organization. The organization is a consolidated reflection of individuals. Same theory works even for competency assessment.

The best part of the assessment is that it objectively shows the areas of focus. This is tremendous contribution to entire Competency Development program. I have seen that this focus helps planning the development activities specific to the competency areas. It reduces the time that participants otherwise have to put-in in 'generic' training programs. It also helps in creating specific case studies and data libraries. This brings in maximum value addition because the libraries are created first, in those areas where there is a maximum need.

0% to 35%		> 35% - 50% <	>50% - 70% <		>70% - 85%<		>85% -100%<
26%	EV anaysis	40%	C'gencies & MR clarity	72%	PM's early involvement
33%	Proj Diary			72%	Cust Tolerence limit
34%	Risk - Prj Objectives	42%	Prj specific reward		
35%	Alternative schedules / strategy sensitization	44%	Informal info for closing	78%	Client interaction frequency
35%	Residual Risk	45%	Correctness - completeness		
		46%	Prj post-mortem		

Further this helps bringing in internal and external mentors specific to the areas identified. The scope of the contribution in the competency development is made very quantitative.

For example, assume that you are a Competency Development manager or HR Manager or Organization Development manager and have been given a task to improve project management maturity in the organization. What all things would you do to determine where do you need to focus? Most of the time, the project managers, their managers are called in and their needs are understood. And, the result of this mostly is the 2 or 3 days training program on "Project Management" under different names like "Fundamentals" or "Advanced" ☺

It is not wrong to get to know their ideas and conduct the training programs. However won't you be happy of participant undergoing training in the specific areas than the generic project management? In such cases, we can either reduce the duration of the program and or we can go deep dive in specifically needed areas in the same available duration for the program.

10.19 Who Can Help Improving These Areas?

"EV Analysis" is the area of utmost focus as shown in the Exhibit 2. In place of generic 2 days program, won't it be value adding if we focus on this specific competency area of EV Analysis?

The mentors internal to the organization are the best resources to improve the competencies. These are the individuals who score 4 or 5 in the competencies under focus.

E.g. there are 2 individuals identified in this organization who scored 5 in the competency "EV Analysis" – Priya and Deepak. It is then these 2 people should be empowered to take the learning further and create the competencies with their other peer project managers. I shall elaborate this point further while describing **"Role of PMO"** in PM Competency Assessment & Development.

26%	EV anaysis	Priya, Deepak
33%	Proj Diary	Bhaven
34%	Risk - Prj Objectives	Milind
35%	Alternative schedules / strategy sensitization	?
35%	Residual Risk	Milind

10.20 The Results

Project Processes (All figures in %)

	Lack of awareness of these processes	Aware but partial and unconfident implementation	Aware of PM & Org. processes but unconfident implementation	Knowledge of PM & Org. processes and confident implementation	Knowledge of PM & Org. processes and proactive implementation
	1	2	3	4	5
Initiating the project	13.33	30.00	20.00	30.00	6.67
Planning the project	0.00	16.67	36.67	36.67	10.00
Executing the project	0.00	0.00	56.67	43.33	0.00
Controlling the project	0.00	10.00	63.33	26.67	0.00
Closing the project	13.33	36.67	46.67	3.33	0.00
Professional Responsibility	0.00	6.67	33.33	36.67	23.33
Organizational Average	**4.44**	**16.67**	**42.78**	**29.44**	**6.67**
Cumulative	4.44	21.11	63.89	93.33	100.00
			63.89	36.11	

1. Project Knowledge Areas

	Lack of awareness of this the knowledge area	Aware but partial and unconfident implementation	Aware of PM & Org. processes but unconfident implementation	Knowledge of PM & Org. processes and confident implementation	Knowledge of PM & Org. processes and proactive implementation
	1	2	3	4	5
Integration Management	6.67	13.33	36.67	20.00	23.33
Scope Management	0.00	0.00	56.67	43.33	0.00
Time Management	0.00	0.00	46.67	50.00	3.33
Cost Management	NA	NA	NA	NA	NA
Quality Management	0.00	26.67	53.33	16.67	3.33
Human Resource Mgmt	0.00	26.67	66.67	6.67	0.00
Communications Mgmt.	3.33	13.33	36.67	46.67	0.00
Risk Management	6.67	46.67	46.67	0.00	0.00
Procurement Management	NA	NA	NA	NA	NA
Organizational Average	**2.38**	**18.10**	**49.05**	**26.19**	**4.29**
Cumulative	2.38	20.48	69.52	95.71	100.00
			69.52	30.48	

10.21 Detailed Quantitative Analysis

After grading the competencies of the participants data collated led to the ranking of the organizational perspective. Here is a representative data of one of the competency assessments that I have done in past.

Analysis Inferences

1. **Project Initiation**

	1	2	3	4	5
Initiating the Project	13.33	30.00	20.00	30.00	6.67
Planning the Project	0.00	16.67	36.67	36.67	10.00
Executing the Project	0.00	0.00	56.67	43.33	0.00
Controlling the Project	0.00	10.00	63.33	26.67	0.00
Closing the Project	13.33	36.67	46.67	3.33	0.00
Professional Responsibility	0.00	6.67	33.33	36.67	23.33
Organizational Average	4.44	16.67	42.78	29.44	6.67

The four participants who exhibited Grade 1 on Project Initiation were three project leaders and one project manager. They were new to their project management role. This problem can be addressed by imparting appropriate training on project management and handholding those new to the PM/PL roles. Far too often the organization encourages a halo effect i.e. it is assumed that one will make a good project manager because an individual is technically sound.

2. **Grades 1 & 2**

	1	2	3	4	5
Initiating the Project	13.33	30.00	20.00	30.00	6.67
Planning the Project	0.00	16.67	36.67	36.67	10.00
Executing the Project	0.00	0.00	56.67	43.33	0.00
Controlling the Project	0.00	10.00	63.33	26.67	0.00
Closing the Project	13.33	36.67	46.67	3.33	0.00
Professional Responsibility	0.00	6.67	33.33	36.67	23.33
Organizational Average	4.44	16.67	42.78	29.44	6.67

All the participants who exhibited competencies at these two grades need to be moved up. Ideally these two grades should have nil occupancy.

3. **Grade 3**

	1	2	3	4	5
Initiating the Project	13.33	30.00	20.00	30.00	6.67
Planning the Project	0.00	16.67	36.67	36.67	10.00
Executing the Project	0.00	0.00	56.67	43.33	0.00
Controlling the Project	0.00	10.00	63.33	26.67	0.00
Closing the Project	13.33	36.67	46.67	3.33	0.00
Professional Responsibility	0.00	6.67	33.33	36.67	23.33
Organizational Average	4.44	16.67	42.78	29.44	6.67

The reason for this high figure (42.78) in Grade 3 here could be any or all of the following.

- The organizational environment does not enable the person to implement best practices.

- The individual's (a) attitude and (b) working style.

- A lack of self-confidence in the subject.

- A lack of ownership in the project.

- A lack of a sense of belonging to the organization.

- What is needed here is a reappraisal of the organizational processes with regards to the type and size of the project so as to avoid complexity in processes.

4. Project Closing

	1	2	3	4	5
Initiating the Project	13.33	30.00	20.00	30.00	6.67
Planning the Project	0.00	16.67	36.67	36.67	10.00
Executing the Project	0.00	0.00	56.67	43.33	0.00
Controlling the Project	0.00	10.00	63.33	26.67	0.00
Closing the Project	13.33	36.67	46.67	(3.33)	0.00
Professional Responsibility	0.00	6.67	33.33	36.67	23.33
Organizational Average	4.44	16.67	42.78	29.44	6.67

Only one person trying to follow standard closing procedures was identified. This could be for the following reasons:

- Transfer of PM to another project even before the formal closing activity is performed.

- Lack of awareness towards positive outputs from project closure.

- Not (well defined) quantified project acceptance criteria.

5. Grade 5

	1	2	3	4	5
Initiating the Project	13.33	30.00	20.00	30.00	6.67
Planning the Project	0.00	16.67	36.67	36.67	10.00
Executing the Project	0.00	0.00	56.67	43.33	0.00
Controlling the Project	0.00	10.00	63.33	26.67	0.00
Closing the Project	13.33	36.67	46.67	3.33	0.00
Professional Responsibility	0.00	6.67	33.33	36.67	23.33
Organizational Average	4.44	16.67	42.78	29.44	6.67

A zero over here is nothing negative. But, it shows a scope for improvement. More and more managers must be proactive and have in themselves the self-initiative to do something more than is expected of them. Please do refer the topics "Role of PMO" [Page 67] and "PMO handling attitudinal issues at Grade 4" [Page 77].

10.22 SkillWillFit Matrix

A quick reference is also possible by SkillFit matrix as mentioned below. It is a schematic diagram.

	Poor PM Skills	Low - medium PM Skills	Medium-High PM Skills	High PM Skills
High Will-Fit				PM 2
Medium Will-Fit				
Low Will-Fit		PM 1		PM 3
Poor Will-Fit	PM 4			

> **REMEMBER: This should NOT be used to Grade an individual. This is first step to identify possible 'mentor(s)'.**

The matrix is filled in based on the total score of rating of all competencies. Higher the consolidated score higher the coordinate of the x-axis. The y axis mentioned about the willingness & attitude.

It does NOT mean that PM4 is no good person. It only means that the person's overall rating on PM is low and this person has also exhibited low interest and willingness in the job of PM. It could be always possible that this person scores extremely good ratings on any one of the 50 competency statements. So even PM4 can be a mentor in the area where the person has scored excellent.

Similarly, it does **NOT** mean the PM2 is excellent in all areas. There are areas where PM2 has scored extremely low. However this person holds good chances to be a good mentor in the areas of his/her expertise.

10.23 Stakeholders Involved & Their Roles

Project Management Competency mapping has the following stakeholders.

Project Managers: Having their competencies accurately mapped out gives project managers a powerful tool for self-diagnosis and a concrete idea of the action that needs to be taken so that they can find most if not all the competencies at a 'Grade 5'.

Top Management: Whether or not an organization has project management competencies mapped out at both individual and organizational grades indicates how serious the top management is on the issue not just as another tool to decide rewards but as a way of growing the organization.

Project Management Office: The project management office has a crucial role to play in competency mapping. These are some of the ways in which the PMO could assist in building competency:

- Generate organization-wide awareness for maintaining the uniformity in the use of project management tool and project schedule structure.

- Impart training to project managers and team members on project management tool(s).

- Provide ongoing assistance to project managers in developing/ tracking project schedules.

- Explore newer project management tools, concepts and methodologies.

- Facilitate simulator for 'would be' PMs.

10.24 Pathways to Solutions

Mapping project management competency is not an end in itself. The organization and the individuals concerned must then engage in actions that will lead to the upgrading of all the competencies of the project managers graded below grade 5.

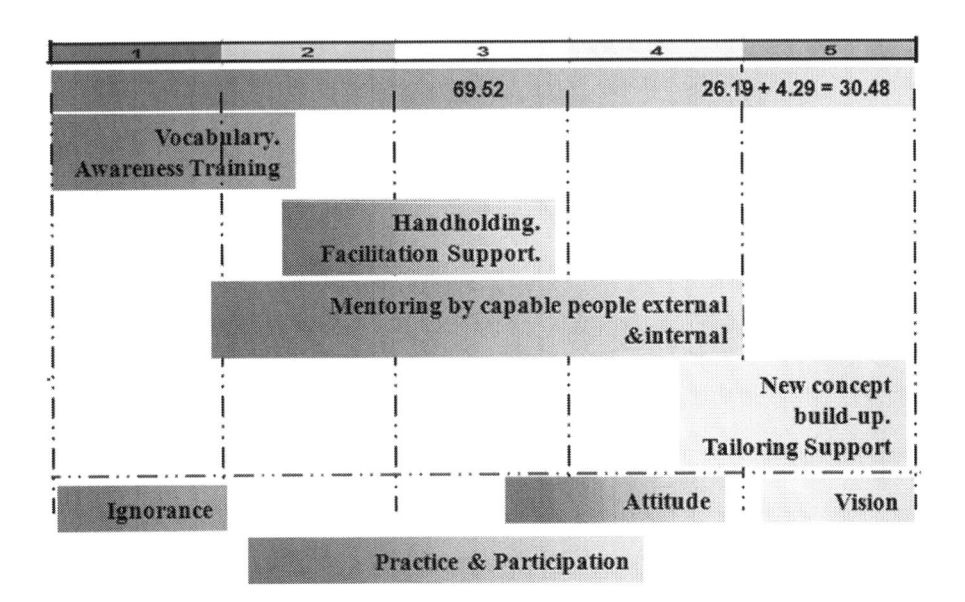

- For subjects graded at grade 1 for different competencies who are essentially battling ignorance, vocabulary awareness training is just what the doctor prescribed.

- Those competencies at grade 2 & 3 are often there because the organizational environment does not enable them to implement best practices. Other reasons could be their lack of self-confidence in the subject and a sense of ownership in the project. For such individuals the organization needs to impart appropriate training on project management and facilitate handholding.

- Project managers at grade 4 are within the striking distance of the summit. All they lack is the right attitude and the vision it takes to be at the top. In such cases, it is difficult to impart generic solutions. What they need instead, is tailor-made support.

- If we want to migrate the project managers exhibiting competencies graded at Grades 1, 2, 3 to Grades 5, then it is unlikely that any external individual or factor can help to great extent. The catalyst for the PM's progress can only come from within the peer group. It is the responsibility of a grade 1–3 PM to seek a mentor from among those of their colleagues more competent than them. At the same time the competent PMs owe it to the organization to mentor those lower on the competency continuum. This most often involves working with a person to help develop one's skills to increase their effectiveness in a specific area. This kind of facilitation must necessarily be offered one on one only. The key to successful mentoring is Trust between mentor and mentee. Needless to say the mentor must NOT be in the chain of command as the mentee.

Please do refer the topics "Role of PMO" [Page 67] and "PMO handling attitudinal issues at Grade 4" [Page 77].

10.25 Role of PMO

This topic will help you connecting the two aspects - PMO and PM Competency Assessment! This topic also serves as a quick revision of the entire content that we have studied so far. Let's have a concise yet concrete revision. This will also help you in mapping the contribution of PMO in PM competency assessment & development.

Basic project management is aimed at answering, "How can we get this project done effectively?" in an ever changing environment.

> *PMO enables answering "How can we make the business more adaptive, responsive and thus more profitable in a rapidly changing multi-project environment?"*

The project management is all about bringing quantitative predictability and visibility in the project endeavor and keeping projects on track with informed decisions about visibility and predictability.

What is PMO?

PMO, in its general parlance, stands for Project or Program Management office. Then, does it mean that the PMO is a separate body? Another island in wonderland of project management?

> *PMO is not a department. Fundamentally PMO is a mindset – a thought process, which helps bringing in quantitative visibility & predictability in projects and programs.*

Of course, one has to set it up as a separate entity mainly for synchronization and facilitation purpose. However, the people contributing in PMO need not be dedicated to PMO. Anyone who has a drive, passion, and ability of bringing quantitative approach in monitoring and forecasting projects and programs can contribute to PMO. So PMO should end up functioning under the guidance principle – by the project managers, of the project managers and for the project managers. ☺ PMO should act as extended body, mind, and intellect of the practicing project managers in the organization.

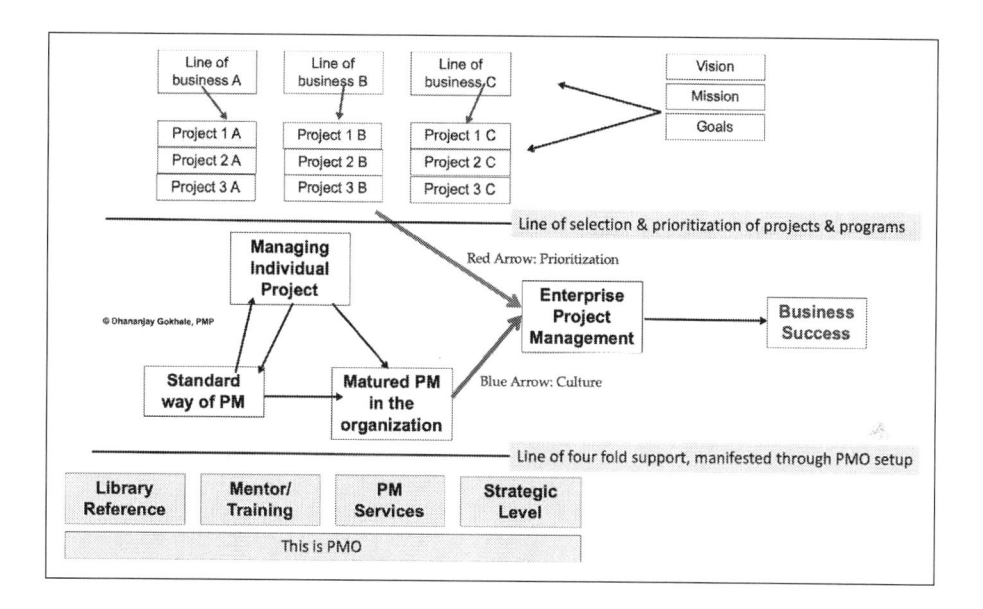

```
┌─────────────────────────────────────────────────────────────────────┐
│   Line of        Line of        Line of           Vision            │
│   business A     business B     business C                          │
│                                                   Mission           │
│   Project 1 A    Project 1 B    Project 1 C       Goals             │
│   Project 2 A    Project 2 B    Project 2 C                         │
│   Project 3 A    Project 3 B    Project 3 C                         │
│                                                                     │
│                              Line of selection & prioritization of projects & programs
│              Managing                                               │
│              Individual      Red Arrow: Prioritization              │
│              Project                                                │
│                              Enterprise                             │
│  © Dhananjay Gokhale, PMP    Project         →    Business          │
│                              Management           Success           │
│                                                                     │
│   Standard      Matured PM    Blue Arrow: Culture                   │
│   way of PM  →  in the                                              │
│                 organization                                        │
│                              Line of four fold support, manifested through PMO setup
│   Library      Mentor/        PM         Strategic                  │
│   Reference    Training       Services   Level                      │
│                     This is PMO                                     │
└─────────────────────────────────────────────────────────────────────┘
```

Let's try to understand the connection between organization and Enterprise Project Management in the organization. Let's refer Exhibit 16. Each organization having crafted its vision, mission, goals, objectives start working on various areas fondly known as Lines Of Business (LOBs). Each LOB has its own vision, mission, and objectives those are planned to achieve by combination of projects, programs, and operations. This is where portfolio management appears in the picture. Project and Program Managers are assigned. They manage individually their projects and programs. They have their own skills and strengths that they bring in to the projects and programs that they manage. Of course here comes a need to make use of each other's strengths. In turn, this starts building up "Standard Way of PM/Best Practices in PM". The two way communication between these two boxes are extremely essential.

While each PM expects the best practices support; it is an individual's duty to contribute to the best practices as well. When we strike a wonderful contributory balance, there emerges "Matured Culture of PM" in the organization.

However, Matured PM Culture is a necessary condition for achieving Enterprise Project Management. However, it is not sufficient. The equally impacting parameter is **prioritization**. Right project at wrong time or wrong project at right time, both are futile. The right project at the right time, that's what clicks. The onus lies with the decision makers or commissioning authority.

Whenever and wherever I have done the PMO establishment exercises, I have focused on 4 aspects that PMO must contribute to as shown in the Exhibit 16.

Library reference, Mentoring/Training, PM Services and Strategic. Let's consider in this way. I generally ask one question to all the PMs. I do it definitely when I conduct PM competency assessment.

<u>As a project manager, what all support do you expect from the organization?</u>

One needs to be ready with the demand statement in case god comes in front and ask, what do you need? I can't afford to fumble and end up demanding something that I do not want.

If god appears and asks, what do you need as a project manager? What are your demands?

I need a cabin. Okay. Done, next? Good chair, good designation, okay. Anything else?

Basically I, as a project or program manager, do not want anybody to do my job, that's for sure. I can do my job and I will do it. I need authority, flexibility, facilities. And I would need your support.

So someone can tell me in case someone has done this kind of a job earlier in our organization. I would need library reference, data. I need history. I need place where I can go and search, view, watch what happened in such kind of projects.

I need somebody who can mentor me. I need someone who can train me. Because there is a lot of incompetence that I have. I know what to do, however not everything I know as to "how to do?" Hence I need somebody to help me knowing. I need somebody to hold my hands.

I don't know how to write risk, I don't understand how to manage people. I don't know how to do the costing? But I try doing my job good, but if somebody can help me there, nothing like it. I would need some services also. Once I know "what to do?" I will start working on it. I would need support to help me doing it.

For example, I will write a risk register and develop a schedule. Can someone at least review those? I might have made 10 mistakes in one estimate. Can someone point those for me? And let's now eliminate each mistake so that I will not make same mistake again. There would be some risks that are not articulated right. There are possibilities that the comprehensiveness of probability and impact analysis is not enough. Fine, I know that I am learning. This is precisely where I would need support.

And last but definitely not the least; can I get strategic level support?

> *If I am claiming something which people generally not very eager to hear to, which lawyer will help me pleading this case and in whose court?*

I am doing it well but sometimes it is not possible. I have analysis and need some different genuine solution for this particular part. So who would like to listen to that? Would Account manager listen that?

Whom shall I go and communicate? Will I get a chance to decide the incoming projects? Will I get a chance to represent PM Community at prioritization stage? Can I put up my case and expressions when a project selected does not seem to have any business connect? Would there be someone to help me stating with quantitative support the fact that I as a project manager am overloaded.

So – library reference, mentoring/training, PM services and Strategic representation are the four areas of support that a PMO should focus on. That's what PMO is all about.

How these PMO services ultimately contribute in PM Competency Assessment and Development?

Assessment: It is definitely PMO's focus to understand the current competency battery in the organization. This falls under "Library Reference" category of the PMO services. This exercise gives the strong data on the state of the PM competencies of current and would be project managers.

Since the assessment exercise also suggests the prioritized list of areas for improvement, the PMO takes it further.

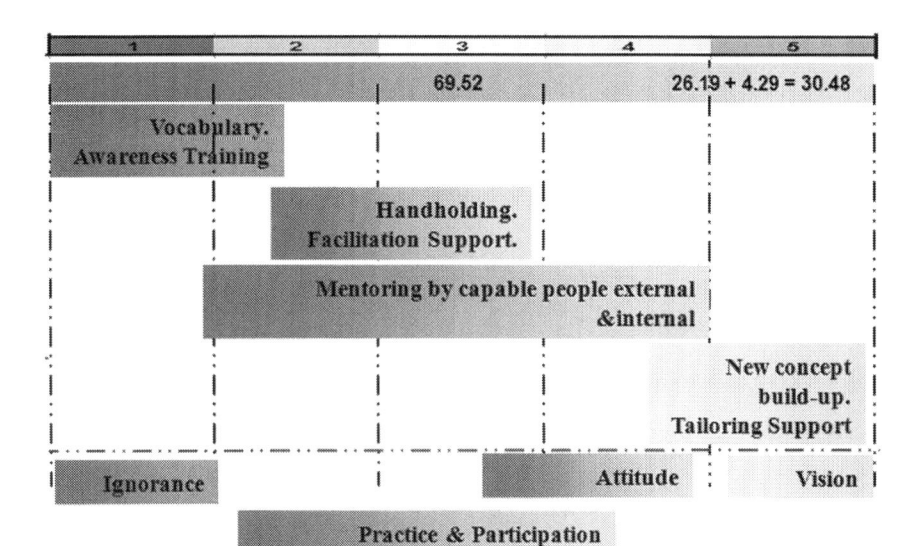

1	2	3	4	5
		69.52	26.19 + 4.29 = 30.48	
	Vocabulary. Awareness Training			
		Handholding. Facilitation Support.		
		Mentoring by capable people external & internal		
				New concept build-up. Tailoring Support
Ignorance			Attitude	Vision
		Practice & Participation		

If you refer the above image, then you would know the 4 pathways to develop the competencies arise out of 4 issues involved.

The four main issues are –

- Ignorance.
- Impediments in practice & participation.
- Attitudinal problems.
- Lack of food for thought/Vision.

These issues are connected to Competency Grades. Further the issues need to be tackled and hence solution strategies are suggested in the exhibit. The following table consolidates all three aspects – issues, grades, and solution strategies.

Issue	Grade	Solution Strategy
Ignorance	1	Awareness build up trainings
Impediments in Practice & Participation	2, 3	Handholding, on the job support, mentoring by internal and external experts.
Attitudinal Problems	4	Engaging into helping others.
Lack of food for thought	5	New concept building, research work, methodology refinements programs. Mentor development.

Now if you relate the "Solution Strategies" to "4 aspects of PMO Contribution" then, it would become extremely clear to appreciate the Role of PMO in competency development. These 4 solutions strategies are the accountabilities of PMO.

Let us consider an example where the competency assessment exercise has inferred that "Risk – Uncertainty" is an area that needs improvement at an organization level. PM Competency assessment also has presented the detailed record on who all are in what grade in this competency. PMO is the internal institute who should have this handy. They must interact with people demonstrating this competency at different grades.

PMO must connect with people scoring Grade 5 for "Risk – Uncertainty". PMO can work on designing and developing the awareness training sessions for those who are scoring Grade 1 in this competency. I always suggest inviting people who have scored Grade 3 in such awareness training program. It is a motivational aspect for both Grade 1 and 3. ☺. Competencies assesses at Grade 3 were once in Grade 1. Over a period intentionally or unintentionally they have moved to this grade of the competency "Risk & Uncertainty". These people can share their experience in Awareness Trainings.

Grade 5 can start working with Grade 2 and 3 helping them in actually performing the job. Their risk registers can be reviewed for uncertainty articulation. What is needed at this Grade is affection ☺ and not auditing! This grade if not handled carefully, can create lot of resistance. The PMO has very important role of a buddy here.

Grade 4 is interesting grade. ☺ PMO can contribute a lot!

> *I always offer "Devil's Advocate" role that suits best to engage anybody who is disinterested.*

People scoring Grade 4 in "Risk – Uncertainty" competency are able to identify the uncertainties in and around project environment, they are able to draft wonderful risk articulations in risk registers, they are able to monitor uncertainties moving to certainties or vice versa.

Then what is the issue involved at this grade? Attitude of 'doing it for the sake' of it even if it needs improvement! People at this Grade 4 exhibit disinterest & indifference to the output of the competency. I always offer them Devil's advocate role to identify the flaws in the process. Further, they are invited to check for possibilities of awareness training program going less contributory. In short they are engaged and over a period of time become extremely important assets for the organization.

Generally Grade 4 is the grade of exit. Many a times, people leaving the organizations are found exhibiting Grade 4 behavior on lots of competencies. It is a clear indication that the person is on look out. Or the person has no other choice and hence continuing in the organization or role somehow for sheer sustenance.

This has impact on SkillWillFit matrix as well. [Refer page 62]. This grade has Skills but Willingness and Fitness may be questionable. Since the person exhibiting Grade 4 in a competency is a strong asset to the organization; it is extremely essential to conserve them. This is the greatest aspect that PMO can contribute to the organization.

> *It is a task pretty similar to brining outcaste community back to societal mainstream* ☺.

The whole idea of competency development is increasing the density in Grade 5. As mentioned, an individual CANNOT be categorized in any grade. It is the competency that gets categorized. So more the competencies available in Grade 5, it means more the possibilities of mentors on those competencies. The habitat of mentors is Grade 5. And major supply to Grade 5 can be developed from Grade 4. It is change in the mind and intellect behavior that we need to bring in Grade 4 appearances.

10.26 PMO Handling Attitudinal Issues at Grade 4

Increasing density at Grade 4 while decreasing density at Grade 5 is definitely a cause for concern. There are two directions to through which Grade 4 density is increased.

- One way is from Grade 3 to Grade 4.
- And another is from Grade 5 to Grade 4.

It is therefore necessary to acknowledge and answer following two questions. The answers to these questions and actions are to be initiated by PMO.

Q 1. Why does a person move from 3 to 4 (& not from 3 to 5)?

Q 2. What makes person moving back from Grade 5 to 4?

Move from Grade 3 to 4

The expected transition is from Grade 3 to Grade 5. There are no impediments left in practice and participation at Grade 3. This grade works very well with mentors and some of them end up developing mentoring skills for the competency at Grade 3. At this grade therefore there is an aspiration to make use of the concepts, search for new techniques, to try maximum compliance with the acquired knowledge and skills. The most important aspect, nevertheless, that can break or make the growth is the reciprocation from the superiors and the overall culture at the organizational level. Imagine a child learning hard way to ride a bicycle. After great efforts, the child learns the riding. And the child, with great enthusiasm and sense of achievement, drives to home where his father welcomes him with sarcastic remark. The child was expecting a wonderful cohesive, nurturing & affectionate expression. Nothing more than that.

> *The feelings that a child carries at this moment are exactly same as those when a person who exhibits a Grade 3 competency gets no appreciation at all.*

The recognition of efforts, achievement and dedication is of utmost important here. If the person is deprived of these three things constantly, then no wonder that the person chooses to exhibit Grade 4 characteristics for the competency under focus. This negative effect does not remain limited to only the competency under focus; however the drive to develop other competencies also takes a hit. The PMO team should be extremely aware about the competencies and their holders at Grade 3. Not even a single instance should be left without acknowledgement and positive push in the form of appreciation. Theory "Whale Done" proposed by Ken Blanchard works very well here!

It is not only the question of appreciation and recognition at the point of achievement. The key moment is to protect and boost at that point where the superior abandons the person tries to improve upon Grade 3 competency but fails. PMO has to genuinely convince them for continuing the efforts. More positively, help the person inferring the learnings even in the event of failure. In fact, the PMO should encourage such people to openly share their failures. This is possible when the value & image of "Failure Sharing" is increased in the organization. I have always ensured that the failure sharing takes place in the PM community of practitioners. Once people understand that learning is appreciated, the courage to work increases. People more openly share their efforts and failure. This sends a clear message to the superiors who react cynically to failure for honest efforts. PMO specifically has two focal points here. PMO must assist the person to prevent or eliminate the mistakes and the damages. Secondly, PMO must appreciate their efforts and drive even if they have failed.

> *And more importantly PMO must work on developing intrinsic awareness of the reasons behind the mistakes made. This creates wisdom from experience.*

This helps developing mentoring and servicing abilities of those people. An alert PMO can definitely increase the throughput of transition from Grade 3 to Grade 5 while reducing the chances of getting trapped at Grade 4.

Move from Grade 5 to 4:

It is also equally interesting to know reasons that make a person moving back from Grade 5 to 4. Fortunately people holding the competencies at Grade 5 have wisely or luckily escaped the Grade 4 trap while moving from Grade 3 to 5.

> *Indeed full marks either to their bravery or to their destiny. ☺ However, the trap at Grade 4 stills remains.*

I have interacted with many people exhibiting few competencies at Grade 4. At least 60% of them have travelled from Grade 5 to 4.

People exhibiting the competencies at Grade 5 are self-motivated people. They are proficient in the competencies at Grade 5. They can and are helping, going out of the way at times, to the people willing to improve the competencies. Grade 5 exhibits the drive for continuous improvement in organizational procedures, tools, and systems levels.

It is therefore surprising to observe the move of competencies from Grade 5 to 4. The main reason was NOT the lack of motivation from anyone but mainly the lack of freedom to try out and going for new possibilities and trying new concepts in project management. If one has to avoid the transitions from 5 to 4; encouragement and empowerment is the main source.

It is said that when your son turns 16, treat him as your friend. So is the case with people exhibiting competencies at Grade 5 ☺

I would share my personal experience. It was way back in 1998. Critical Chain project management (CCPM) – a concept based on Theory of Constraint was a point of fascination for me that time. There was not any organization in India then that has gone ahead with CCPM, at least to my knowledge. I strongly believed that this concept will work. It is more to do with the human beings and their psyche than scheduling. ☺ I was heading PMO in one of the IT organizations then. I decided to try out on new project starting with a client in UK. The project manager was a very good friend of mine.

PMO has to be in the list of 'good friends' of PMs.☺

That PM had many competencies listed at Grade 5. It goes without saying that the PM was exhibiting Grade 5 behavior on many of those competencies. A person had a drive & passion. Of late, nevertheless there were some glimpses of mental travel from Grade 5 to 4 on couple of competencies. The reason mainly was non-approvals for trying out new things. This time I had made up my mind. With the awareness of the chief of the department; I invited him to check his willingness for implementing CCPM. I knew he would be more than happy. I was still curious to observe him. His body language responded enthusiastically during the chat. However in the beginning; there was a glimpse of that downward travel. "I definitely want to do it. In fact I have been working on estimating patterns and human natures involved in efforts and duration estimating", he said; "anyways, it seems that it is not needed in organization now" followed by light sarcasm. I was happy that I initiated this move at right time.

"Look, this project is in limelight. And the Account Manager wants to try few innovative things. I had a word with him. Your manager was initially skeptical; however it was totally due to misnomers about CCPM concept. Now, when I explained the simplicity and practicality of this concept, he is looking forward for it as there are many advantages that are sought. I am sure with your support we can implement CCPM. Can we help each other☺?" – I checked.

"Yes Of course" – he answered flamboyantly☺.

The CCPM implementation went extremely well.

- More than that we saved Grade 5 competencies getting trapped into Grade 4.
- Most importantly, this person further helped doing the same with some other people.
- The individuals and the organization both are the beneficiaries.

Here ends the chapter 10. This chapter describes a very important contribution of the PMO. In fact, the very existence of the PMO is for this function - Assessing & developing the PM Competency in the organization.

The entire exercise of mapping project management competency might add little lasting value to the organization, if the right mindset is not in place amongst the various stakeholders. What are needed are honest efforts at improvement whether it is at the grade of the project manager or at the grade of the organization that employs.

Often competency mapping runs the risk of being just another new-fangled process that happens to be the flavor of the season. Such a powerful organizational tool is often resorted just because rival organizations have implemented it and not because there is genuine appreciation of its benefits. In such instances one finds management pressures to grade as many PMs as high as possible thus are defeating the very purpose of the exercise. Project Management Competency mapping should not be seen as just another means to apportion and dispense rewards.

All the stakeholders must see, in the exercise, an opportunity for long-term growth. The key is to look at project management competency mapping as going beyond mere processes. And to see in it an exercise that has a significant and lasting value to project managers as well as to the organization.

Before moving to the next chapter, let's take a small quiz.

Section A: Fill in the Blanks

1. The objective of the Project Manager is to _____.

2. _____ is one of the basic instincts of human being.

3. PM Competency _____ is a very first step in developing competency through _____ _____ of the project managers.

4. Project management is an art of _____.

5. _____, _____, and _____ is a tripod of competency.

6. The MBTI model mainly preferences on 4 areas. They are,

   a. _____ & Extraversion.

   b. Sensing & _____.

   c. Thinking & _____.

   d. _____ & Perceiving.

7. SkillWillFit Matrix should be used as a first step to PM Competency _____.

8. The key stakeholders involved in the Project Management Competency mapping are _____, _____, and _____ at the very least.

9. Fundamentally PMO is a _____, which helps bringing in _____ _____ & _____ in projects and programs.

10. The four main issues in developing PM competency are.

    a. _____.   b. _____.

    c. _____.   d. _____.

Section B: Open/Narrative questions:

1. State two possible reasons behind the misconception set regarding the objective of the PM, in the industry?

2. List 5 responsibilities of the PM.

3. Why is it necessary to perform the competency assessment before moving to the competency development?

4. Project management is an art of compromise. True or False. Explain with example.

5. Why does the author pass a remark – "Project Management is all about pulling strings☺"

6. Define Competency and its aspects.

7. Are competencies innate and static? Justify.

8. What is the tripod of competency?

9. What are the constituents of Project Management Competency? List the competencies giving example with any one knowledge area or project phase.

10. Project Management competencies involve professional and personal competencies. Throw the light on the statement.

11. Is it a good idea to grade a person? How can a person be graded on the basis on his/her competencies. Explain briefly.

12. What are different grades of PM competency scale? How are they useful in grading the person as PM?

13. Give a real life example in your domain area to explain how an individual matures through the different grades of PM competency. Use the grades explained in the book.

14. In what scenarios do you feel that the personal interview is the method of choice?

15. Why the author emphasized on the method and what are the benefits received?

16. The PM assessment model explained in the case study can be applied to assess any person from any domain area. True or False? Justify by giving example in one domain.

17. While performing a face to face interview, what all points did author take care? Why it is important to give attention to these points? What will be the impact on the outcome of the interview if these points are missed?

18. Why do you think there are tough behaviors? What all tough behaviors have you observed in your professional or personal life while performing a direct communication?

19. With the help of the points explained, how can you change your strategy to get the expected output from the communication? Explain with illustration.

20. What are different personality types? How a personality type is linked with the person's behavior? Explain with one example.

21. Exercise: You are going to have a one on one communication with a person with **INFJ** personality type. What homework will you do before the meeting? List down your approaches or helping points.

22. What are the basic foundations of the communication?

23. What all areas of competencies are explained? Do you think that all these areas are required for competency assessment? Discuss.

24. The author has discussed points about the analysis and the consolidation of the collected data. Discuss the methodology and comment on the benefits of such analysis at the organizational level.

25. Why generic training program is not always a good option for competency development?

26. What is SkillWillFit Matrix? How it can be used to choose the mentors in different areas?

27. Most of the time the organizational project management competency can be improved within the peer group without any external training or mentoring. Assess the statement.

28. Typically what should be PMO competencies? List down and briefly explain in which areas the PMO can act as helping hand or mentor.

29. Discuss the link between competency issues, individual and organizational competency grades, and the solution strategy for competency development. How PMO functions contribute in this scenario?

30. Why do you think that an increasing density of Grade 4 density is a point of concern? Discuss reasons of developing this situation and the ways for improvement.

For premium exclusive videos, visit https://vimeo.com/ondemand/pmowonderland or contact us at dg@dgonline.in for special discounted prices, quizzes, & 12 PDUs.

Chapter 11

The Position & Potential Issues

We are learning the concepts and implementation aspects of project and program management office set up. We have travelled 10 chapters by now.

We have seen the wonder perspective, roaming buffalos, need for ambidexterity and we have also pulled 63 strings! We focused on the fundamental connection between project & program management with PMO in the earlier chapter.

We saw one real life example of a senior leader demanding the PMO for the name-sake. We then listed the characteristics of the name-sake PMO.

We also understood the 4 baskets of the PMO support. We also enlisted and elaborated the functions of PMO. We elaborated the most important role of the PMO – Competency Development!

We also had a deep dive into PM competency assessment & development with the help of my book.

Let me now welcome you to 11th Chapter – The position & issues! Now let's define the PMO's position in the organization structure & issues involved while setting the PMO.

What could be the PMO position? PMO is an institution that needs to be adaptive. The PMO exists through its 'four-baskets' support. The support can be at work package level, or at sub-project level, or project, mega-project, program or even at the business unit level. The position therefore must be adaptive.

> *The presence and the function of PMO is independent of the project and program size and complexity.*

As we say, PMO is a center that provides four-folded support. This support is needed for project & program manager of a smallest and simplest to largest & complex projects & programs. The areas of support remains same. The efforts contributed will vary depending upon the size, complexity and most importantly the competency of the project or program manager.

All the four-folded support can be provided either by one person or set of people. These people can be within the project or program team or can be dedicated exclusive team or it could be centralized team supporting on all four fronts library, mentoring, services, and strategy which will take care of ignorance, practice and participation, attitude, and vision.

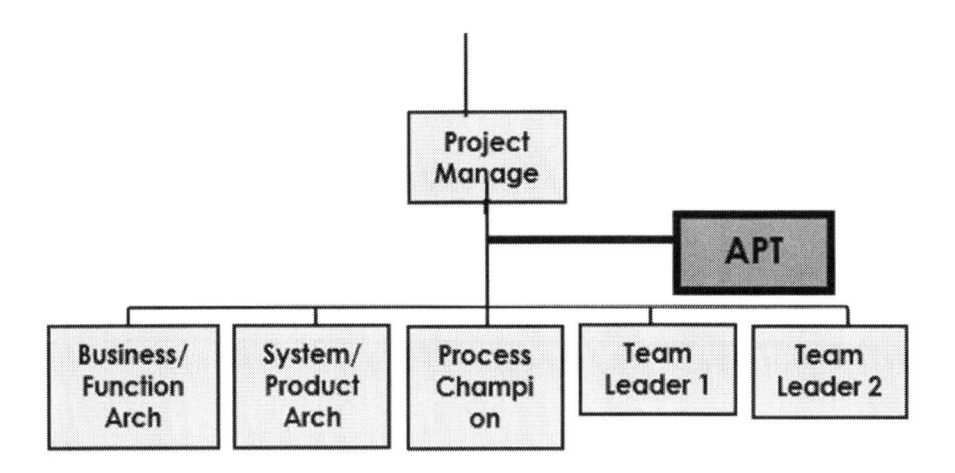

```
                    Project
                    Manage
                       |
                       +----------------------- APT
                       |
   +----------+----------+----------+----------+
Business/   System/    Process    Team       Team
Function    Product    Champi    Leader 1   Leader 2
Arch        Arch        on
```

PMO can exist for a project, or for group of projects. When the PMO works dedicatedly for the given project or a program it is known as **APT – Autonomous Project or Program Team!**

PMO can exist for a program, for a group of programs or it can be at domain or the business level. The position of the PMO should be

Staff Function, irrespective type and size of the PMO. Neither PMO should report to Project & Program Managers nor do they report to PMO. PMO people should NEVER be made responsible or accountable for the delivery.

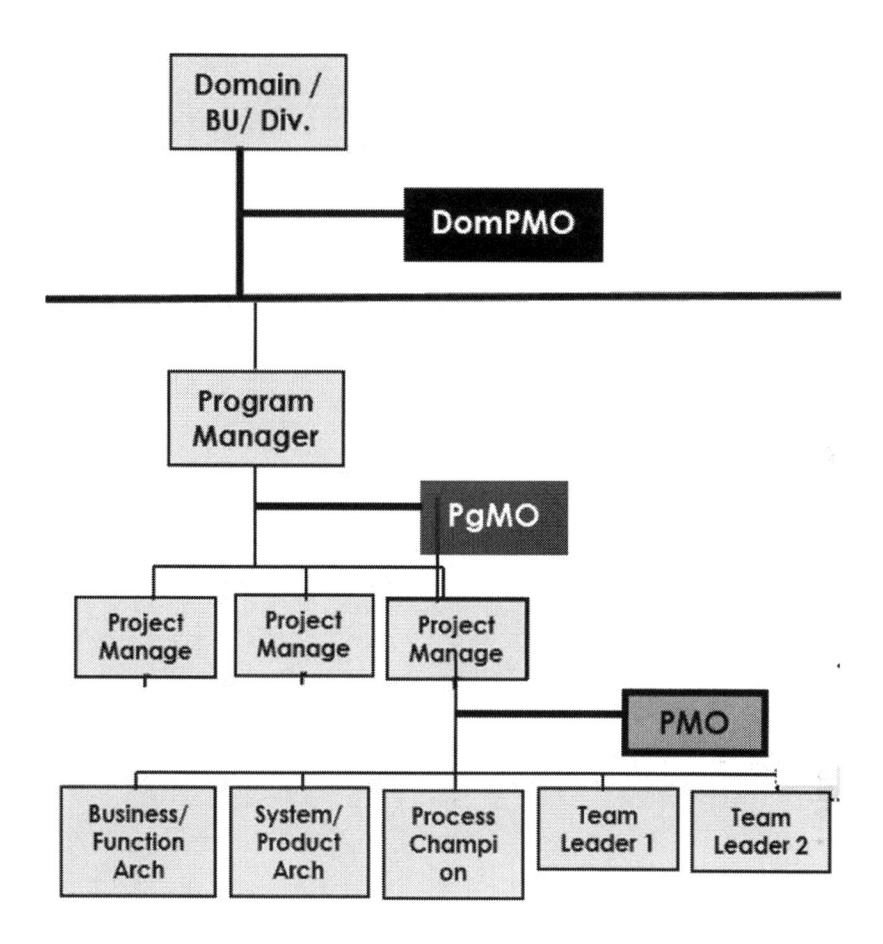

```
           ┌──────────────┐
           │  Domain /    │
           │  BU/ Div.    │
           └──────┬───────┘
                  ├──────────────┬─────────────┐
                  │              │   DomPMO    │
                  │              └─────────────┘
           ┌──────┴───────┐
           │   Program    │
           │   Manager    │
           └──────┬───────┘
                  ├──────────────┬─────────────┐
                  │              │    PgMO     │
                  │              └─────────────┘
      ┌───────┬───┴───┬───────┐
      │       │       │       │
  ┌───┴──┐┌───┴──┐┌───┴──┐
  │Project││Project││Project│
  │Manager││Manager││Manager│
  └──────┘└──────┘└───┬──┘
                      ├─────────────┬─────────────┐
                      │             │    PMO      │
                      │             └─────────────┘
  ┌─────────┬─────────┼─────────┬─────────┐
  │Business/││System/ ││Process ││ Team   ││ Team   │
  │Function ││Product ││Champi- ││Leader 1││Leader 2│
  │  Arch   ││  Arch  ││  on    │
```

However that does not mean that PMO members should exhibit careless or dis-owned behavior towards the projects and program. On the contrary, the PMO members should take enthusiastic initiative to help project & program managers on all four fronts. More importantly, this should be based on intrinsic willingness.

Not all the aspects are simple and hurdle free. There exist few issues in setting up PMO.

So what could be the potential issues involved in this setup?

Issue 01 – Lack of respect: "Will you be ready to leave your current project or program manager position for next 3 years and devote your time totally in facilitating skill-based training programs in organization?" The basic issues is lack of respect. It starts with lack of respect for self, and then the lack of respect for the role or the job that is being done. This is seen not only in PMO. This issue is also seen in other support or non-limelight fields as well.

> *"Will you be ready to leave your current project or program manager position for next 3 years and devote your time totally in facilitating skill-based training programs in organization?"*

"Will you be ready to leave your current project or program manager position for next 3 years and devote your time totally in facilitating skill-based training programs in organization?" I have asked this question to many senior people. People are reluctant. I have experienced it. Why? Because one has to leave the delivery side or to leave the area of power. It's a lack respect for self. I was a project manager, program manager. And now? I am a PMO member. Powerful Designation will not be there. It is the lack of respect given to the PMO role by existing mindset of the people in the organizations. My designation will be PMO member, at the most PMO Officer or best is Chief PMO. It does not make sense much to me and then to the world around.

Issue 02 – Overhead Mentality: The services provided (existence of the project office) is considered as an overhead or a heavy baggage that one has to carry for no reason. Project office neither involved since project initiation, nor involved in project review meetings. Senior Managers many times are interested only in reports. Hence PMOs are not kept intimated about the start of the new projects.

Issue 03 – Resources and capabilities:

As we discussed earlier in this learning intervention, the people forming the PMO and therefore people joining the PMO lack the fundamental understanding of the skills requirement for performing PMO functions. The number and quality of the resources made available for the PMO is always much less than required. The major reason is that PMO is considered as a cost center. People forget that they should consider it as Investment Center so that return can be expected. Many times, good resources are denied due to cost constraints.

Lack of respect for self and lack of respect for the PMO function creates the scarcity for the PMO resources. To add to it, lack of budget further deteriorates the situation.

The people joining the PMO should have some basic set of competencies. It is essential to build these competencies in PMO members first. A person should be able to project reality, should have courage to speak truth, should be process oriented, should have service orientation.

Issue 04 – Lack of service orientation: PMO is fundamentally a staff function. It is like a service industry. PMO is there to provide services from the 4 baskets. This needs the service orientation, the mindset of offering services. One must not forget that the PMO gets the treatment of step-child. The PMO members must win the confidence and trust of the other key stakeholders. It is possible only through providing all legitimate services to project & program managers whole-heartedly.

Who are the customers for PMO? Project & program managers. And surprisingly who are the strong resistors for the PMO? Again project & program managers.

So, when a customer is a strong resistor, only technique that works is service.

Issue 05 – Lack of concept selling skills. You have to sale the PMO, its thought process, its concepts to the people in the organization. There are mainly three sets of people in the organization in the context to PMO.

One, the people who are not at all aware about the concept and hence absolutely neutral about this activity.

Second, the people who mis-understand the PMO and hence are the resistors.

The third category is of the people who know and are supporters. The sales & marketing skills are required to tackle the 1st and 2nd category. The 1st category needs to be provided with an education about the PMO. It should be in a lively manner and concerting neutrals to supporters.

The second category is tougher. They are like the customers who are totally against a certain brand. It is a tough time for the sales person to bring them back. The patience and demonstrations of advantages at right time are the two skills necessary for PMO members.

But it is observed that the PMO members lack on these skills. I have always considered this aspect of utmost importance and whenever and wherever I have set up the PMOs, I ensured that there are couple of people associated with PMO who are extremely good in spreading the word in addition to the promotional activities. Each person working in and for PMO must have marketing and selling attitude. They must appreciate & speak about the value proposition that PMO brings to the organization. They must propagate the contributory activities that PMO does. They must publish the benefits of PMO sought by people or department. There is no selfish interest involved in doing so.

Issue 06 – Lack of Senior Management support: Many times, the PMO set up activities are considered as pre-requisite for new orders. Even then they are considered as overheads. And hence the support from the senior management is shaky. The management must show patience while checking the deliverables from PMO. Other follow the leaders. If the senior management through its speech and behavior are not respecting the PMO, then others will also start taking the PMO lightly. This makes the PMO's job further difficult.

Issue 07 – Lack of commitment from PMO members: PMO members' commitment of time is very essential. If the wrong candidate is selected for PMO work then it is a damage to the PMO. Setting up a Contributory PMO is a process that needs patience and perseverance. Hence minimum 15 to 18 months' time commitment is expected from the members joining the PMO team.

Issue 08 – Vague Career Path for the PMO members: The commitment of the PMO members also depends up on one more factor. It is the career path. Say a team member invests 1.5 to 2 years of his career in PMO. What would be the next step or phase for the person?

The team in the PMO is always of varied skills and experiences. We need people from fresher to practitioner. Experience ranges from 1 to 15 years or sometime more. For supporting on strategy basket, people we would need senior members. While for library basket, a person with 1 yr. experience is good enough. We should have clear career path for all the members. The career path has two options – growth within the PMO or growth outside the PMO.

The ultimate transformational step in the life of PMO is that a cost center PMO transformed to the profit center PMO providing chargeable PM Professional Services. As we will list the characteristics of the contributory PMO later, we will touch up this point. With this transformation coming true, the opportunities for performing people has no dearth.

Issue 09 – Unavailability of the tools and infrastructure: A good PMO will never insist on purchasing the high end tools and state of the art infrastructure. Developing the mindset is the first step. Automation without matured processes and matured mindset is always dangerous. Nevertheless there is a need of minimum infrastructure like place, discussion room, consulting room, and communication tools. Many a times it is observed that these basics are also denied under the cause of budget constraints. This again goes back to the senior management's look out and support to PMO.

Setting up the contributory PMO is all about acting and eliminating these issues. Of course, this is not an overnight trip. It needs systematic, planned, and tenacious efforts. Managing people is the key aspect in setting the PMO. Now that we have acknowledged and appreciated the issues involved in PMO, let's now move to setting the ball rolling. However, before that let's understand the characteristics of the contributory PMO. We will enlist and elaborate the characteristics of contributory PMO in the next chapter.

Before moving to the next chapter, let's take a small quiz.

Mark the Statements True or False

1. The presence and the function of PMO is dependent of the project and program size and complexity.

2. This support from PMO is needed for project & program manager of a larger & complex projects & programs.

3. When the PMO works dedicatedly for the given project or a program it is known as APT.

4. Irrespective type and size of the PMO, the position of the PMO should be Staff Function.

5. "Lack of self-respect & lack of respect for the PMO function" creates the scarcity for the PMO resources.

6. PMO members need not have marketing and selling attitude as basically the marketing function is a distinct and separate function than PMO.

7. Project & Program managers are the key resistors of the PMO set up endeavour initially.

8. Since PMO members initially are not held accountable for the delivery, they need not worry about it.

9. If the senior management does not invite PMO during key planning and review meetings for projects and programs, then PMO members should not go to such meetings.

10. Service orientation attitude and corresponding actions help in winning the confidence of the stakeholders.

11. If we need to increase the willingness of competent person to join the PMO, then there must be a very clear career path defined.

For premium exclusive videos, visit https://vimeo.com/ondemand/pmowonderland or contact us at dg@dgonline.in for special discounted prices, quizzes, & 12 PDUs.

Chapter 12

The Contributory PMO

We are learning the concepts and implementation aspects of project and program management office set up. We have travelled 11 chapters by now.

We have seen the wonder perspective, roaming buffalos, need for ambidexterity and we have also pulled 63 strings! We focused on the fundamental connection between project & program management with PMO in the earlier chapter.

We saw one real life example of a senior leader demanding the PMO for the name-sake. We then listed the characteristics of the name-sake PMO.

We also understood the 4 baskets of the PMO support. We also enlisted and elaborated the functions of PMO. We elaborated the most important role of the PMO – Competency Development!

We also had a deep dive into PM competency assessment & development with the help of my book.

We have elaborated on the organizational position & issues involved while setting the PMO.

Let me now welcome you to 12th Chapter – This is the right time to enlist the characteristics of the Contributory PMO.

Vision of PMO: Organization without PMO.

> *Organization without a PMO.*

This entire learning intervention is about setting up the Contributory PMO, and the vision of contributory PMO is "Organization without PMO". Isn't this vision statement contradictory? There is no contradiction at all. Organization without PMO is the ultimate stage where there is no NEED to have any manifested PMO. The PMO has become the second nature. PMO is not a physical entity. It is a mind-set. It is way of working. Once the mind-set of contributory PMO is adopted across the organization, there is no need to have separate PMO. Each individual behaves and lives it. Contributory PMO drives to achieve it.

Value Proposition:

> *How can we make the business more adaptive, responsive and thus more profitable in a rapidly changing environment.*

The name-sake PMO has a value proposition of some temporary, looking & feeling good excitement. Whereas the contributory PMO focus on business side. It contributes to whole business making it profit making. We have dealt with this perspective earlier in this learning intervention.

Recruitment Criteria for Contributory PMO staff: Dedicated, 'Been there...done that!', Mentoring Ability, Service Orientation, Commitment – min 2 years.

The people working for contributory PMO need to have 24 by 7 dedication. They should be able to hold the hands of the one interested and also of those who are not. Contributory PMO members are the change agents or transformation agents. They transform the entire organization into more predictable conditions. A person should be able to project reality, should have courage to speak truth, should be process oriented, should have service orientation.

Hidden agenda of the people joining: There is no hidden agenda. People joining the contributory PMO are joining with clear awareness of the efforts & risks involved. They are aware about the commitment needed.

Reporting to: Project or Program Manager; Domain or Business Head; MD, CEO, or a Strong strategic sponsor. The contributory PMO has very clear reporting authority. There exists a strong strategic sponsor.

Chart of accounts: It is looked at as development of profit center in the form of Project & Program Management Professional Service provider department. Investment (to be followed up with Returns). Unlike the name-sake PMO, the money spent on the Contributory PMO is considered as Investment. And hence the strategic sponsor has a keen eye on the returns. I personally always felt happy whenever such a tracking is done by the strategic sponsor. It shows that it matters to the organizations. The advantage of this approach is that the Contributory PMO is not considered as a Cost Center.

It is looked at as development of profit center in the form of Project & Program Management Professional Service provider department.

A very clear budget is demanded from the PMO chief. And since it is a budget it is connected to tangible deliverables.

Competency Required: Analytical Skills, Assertiveness, Service orientation, and consulting attitude. We have dealt with this aspect in earlier parts in this learning intervention. The people joining the

PMO should have some basic set of competencies. It is essential to build these competencies in PMO members first. A person should be able to project reality, should have courage to speak truth, should be process oriented, should have service orientation.

KRA & KPA: Develop equally, if not more competent successor!

KRA stands for Key Result Area while KPA stands for Key Performance Area. The dream of the contributory PMO is to have a sustainable development of the project & program management mind-set across the organization. KPA/KRA determined for the PMO members is that they have to develop more competent successor. For example, **'Schedule Developer'** is one of the key roles that I develop when I set up the PMOs. The responsibility of this role is to thoroughly seek the mastery over the scheduling tools, thoroughly seek the inputs of the scheduling strategy, and assist in developing the schedule to project manager. As one of the KRAs, in addition to other responsibilities, is that this person must develop at least one successor equally or higher competent.

There are two advantages of this KRA.

One, the PMO gets an additional bandwidth as PMO's work start increasing. It also acts as a backup.

The second advantage is that the person who transforms skills to successors, gets to do some more responsibility in turn growing up or laterally in the organization.

Organization Position: As we saw in earlier model, the PMO position should be a staff function. The contributory PMO is placed as a staff position. In addition to that any interferences from any other stakeholder is not accepted when it comes to data analysis and presentation with recommendations and actions. The contributory PMO has very clear connect to Project & Program Management Team as well as to the strategic sponsor. However this does not get confused as a dual reporting. Because the reporting always remains to the strategic sponsor.

Career Path: PM Professional Service Provider.

The people performing as PMO member, must have very clear career path. We elaborated this in the earlier chapter. The contributory PMO has clear Career Paths decided. A very clear career path is getting into a role of Project & Program Management professional service provider. A person performing with due diligence in any role in the contributory PMO can move into consulting role pertaining to the area of competency. This is applicable to any role in PMO. In fact, this brings in the Profit Centre status to the Contributory PMO.

Fate: Profit Center, New Line of Business

The contributory PMO initially starts providing the services in all 4 baskets to some select projects and programs. We will deal with this when we will work on actions necessary for the setting up PMO. Later, the purview of the Contributory PMO is increased to many more projects and programs. And ultimately all the projects, programs and portfolios happening in the organizations come under the support baskets of the PMO. The same support services can be provided to other sister concerns, group companies or other organizations outside in the industry.

Once this starts, the Contributory PMO starts as a Profit Centre because the services provided for are charged. Many times, with very high maturity, the services are charged internally as well.

Set-up Time: 8 to 10 months at org level set up.

Now that we have gone through the characteristics of the Contributory PMO, you would appreciate that to reach this stage it would need at least 8 to 10 months of dedicated efforts. This is worth.

The organization without PMO!

This is the dream!

Before moving to the next chapter, let's take a small quiz.

Mark the Statements True or False

1. 'Organization without PMO' means that we should not spend money on setting up the PMO.
2. 'Organization without PMO' means that each individual behaves like a contributory PMO.
3. Vision of the contributory PMO is to have more profit.
4. Value proposition of the contributory PMO is to give PM services at least cost possible.
5. Minimum commitment required by an individual is 2 months.
6. The fate of the contributory PMO is to transform itself to the profit centre by becoming a line of business – a professional service provider.
7. There should not be any interference to PMO when it comes to data presentation and third party analysis of the projects and programs in the organization being done.
8. The program managers must report to PMO Chief.
9. The project Manager must report to PMO Chief.
10. The PMO should report to project manager.
11. APT should report to project manager.

For premium exclusive videos, visit https://vimeo.com/ondemand/pmowonderland or contact us at dg@dgonline.in for special discounted prices, quizzes, & 12 PDUs.

Chapter 13

Set the Ball Rolling

We are learning the concepts and implementation aspects of project and program management office set up. We have travelled 12 chapters by now.

We have seen the wonder perspective, roaming buffalos, need for ambidexterity and we have also pulled 63 strings! We focused on the fundamental connection between project & program management with PMO in the earlier chapter.

We saw one real life example of a senior leader demanding the PMO for the name-sake. We then listed the characteristics of the name-sake PMO.

We also understood the 4 baskets of the PMO support. We also enlisted and elaborated the functions of PMO. We elaborated the most important role of the PMO – Competency Development!

We also had a deep dive into PM competency assessment & development with the help of my book.

We have elaborated on the organizational position & issues involved while setting the PMO. We elaborated the characteristics of the Contributory PMO.

Let me now welcome you to 13th Chapter –Now let's move forward and get to know few tips for implementing the PMO.

Tip 01 – Acknowledge and appreciate the need and presence of PMO:

The very first step is to start spreading the word about setting up the PMO. The most important is that one should never use the word PMO. Isn't it interesting?

To spread the word without using the word!

The crucial mistake that takes place in this step is that the owner announces that the PMO is being set in the organization. This creates resistance. Instead, I always suggest the leader to keep an introductory session on PM Competency Assessment, or Critical Chain Project Management, or Wonderlands of Project & Program Manager, etc. The essential part of this initial session is to create interest, eagerness and curiosity through entertainment. Many a times I facilitate half a day "PM Sensitization Workshop". Any of such topics has always helped me. This kind of presentation or facilitation helps in making the participants feel & appreciate the need of such systematic approach that can be brought in through an entity that world calls as PMO.

> *I never remember, in last 16 years, me announcing or letting anybody announce that we are beginning for PMO.*

Tip 02 – Formally initiate the PMO setup as a project with a strong sponsor in the organization. Budget specifically for the resource!

It may seem that the 1st and the 2nd steps are contradictory. Earlier, I suggested that never declare that you are starting the PMO setup exercise. While here, the suggestion is to initiate the PMO Set Up project formally. How is it possible? The name "PMO" is kept confidential only to two people – the strategic sponsor and the project manager of the exercise. Of course as a consultant, I have been always kept informed.

Most commonly so far DG has named this project as "Schedule Management Service Set Up" or "Building project & program management competencies". Such nomenclature increases the interest of the stakeholders. The expected resistance to PMO is reduced. It is the simple name with least possible perception possibilities. The PMO word creates lots of perception. This is where we started our learning intervention. PMO as Wonder!

Tip 03 – Sensitize PM <> PMO <> Business Heads interactions!

Remember never say that you are setting up a PMO. Once we roll out the project under the name "Schedule Management Service Set Up", the key stakeholders are the project & program managers. On the background of initial edutainment (education with entertainment) session, participants' interest levels are increased. And hence when we set up a roll-out meeting, an opportunity arises as most of the people ask "what exactly would you do?"; "would you be developing our schedules?", "we anyway develop it and then why do you need this services?" All these questions are really important that gives you ample opportunity to present the expected outputs.

At this time present the complete strategy – right from defining the "role of schedule assistant" to "expected sitting arrangement for the project review meetings".

Schedule is most vital and most taken for granted artefact in the project & program management. Schedule is a throughput diagram. And once a reliable throughput diagram is drawn, the corner stone is laid. This gives opportunity to set the facilitated meetings between Project-Program Managers, the PMO team and the senior management.

Remember never say that you are setting up a PMO.

Tip 04 – Start setting with 3 to 4 small projects OR 1 large project:

The schedule management services should be kicked off for 3 to 4 smaller projects of say 3 to 5 months duration. Or it can be kicked off for 1 to 2 larger projects or programs of around 12 to 15 months. I prefer going for more number of smaller projects or programs than lesser number of larger projects. This provides opportunity to spread the word actively to more teams.

Schedule management service gives opportunity to PMO team to initiate 2nd and 3rd baskets simultaneously. The 2nd basket is about mentoring and training, while the 3rd basket is about services – review, development, validation, assistance, etc. When this service starts, the interactions start. The PMO member – schedule assistant, or schedule developer and schedule architect starts interacting with project or program managers, the key team members, and some experts.

The initial phase is skeptical. People don't tend to trust the PMO members. This is where the connecting and collaborating skills with service orientation of PMO members come handy. Once the skepticism phase is crossed, there comes a phase were patience is tried. As the schedule is developed more detailed discussions on the deliverables, activities, efforts, productivity, duration, sequencing, what-if analysis, and execution strategy are opened up. This is indeed a delicate time.

PMO members needs to be extremely careful in maneuvering the discussions. Of course, once the team starts seeing a robust schedule developed and once the teams understand the benefits of what-ifs being done; there comes a sigh of confidence. This is where the first glimpse of acceptance of PMO through intrinsic willingness of the projects and program teams are seen. Remember even now, we are not calling this as a PMO.

Tip 05 – People – select the people. Been there, done that, ready to support.

The people working for contributory PMO needs absolutely 24 by 7 dedication. They should be able to hold the hands of interested people and also of those who are not. Contributory PMO members are the transformation agents. They transform the entire organization to more predictable and adoptive conditions. A person should be able to project reality, should have courage to speak truth, should be process oriented, should have service orientation.

This is a very crucial step. One needs to create interest and attraction amongst few right candidates about the PMO. This is not enough, it is more complicated to get them relieved from their current duties. We cannot afford to have all PMO members working part time in PMO. My experience says 2 to 3 members working full time is sufficient to being with. We are starting small so here the organization size does not impact.

Sensitize the team well. Make them aware about all the tough times and hard reactions that they might have to face in their role. Ensure that the service orientation is not missed.

Tip 06 – Plan for buying in phase – handle the objections, apprehensions empathetically:

PMO set up is more of a psychological forte. It is a mind-set transformational activity. There would be resistance for any new change. Most surprisingly, the resistance for the PMO is put-up from the community of project and program managers. This looks tricky.

In the year 1998, when it was the first time I was setting up the PMO internally for one of the reputed organizations, in Athens, Greece. I had assumed that Project and Program Managers would definitely support me because the services that we have planned to offer are for the benefit of them. However I was amazed to see their reactions. One of the senior project manager with his colleague openly asked, "Why you and your PMO team is needed?" He did not hesitate to comment further "You will be additional headache for us."

Later, I could realize that the project and the program managers are bogged down by non-contributory audits and when they need help they are shown non-conformance notices.

They expect someone to help them and not audit them.

Well, that was the beginning. And I found that this resistance can be transmuted to cooperation. And my plan was in line with that.

Tip 07 – Set and follow the rhythm!

Setting up the contributory PMO, is a test of one's patience. To add to it, it also needs delicacy. There are lot of activities that one needs to accomplish. Some of them are one time activities or lesser frequency activities, while some of them are regular, higher frequency activities. Identification of physical office, recruiting the base team, are the examples of the first type. While maintaining the team's moral, interactive discussions with project and program managers, assistance on schedule development activities, reviews of the projects and programs, are the examples of the second type of activities.

These frequent tasks are extremely essential. It is therefore advisable to set the rhythm for these activities. And of course, once planned, we need to follow the rhythm. Setting the rhythm and following it; helps in generating the confidence in the stakeholders. It reduces the reverse journey which is very quick in such kind of endeavours. It brings in discipline in activities that are essential for project and program management.

Tip 08 – Understand the phases of implementation – avoid killing the hen that lays the golden eggs.

Like I said, setting up the contributory PMO is a delicate tasks that needs patience and perseverance.

It is a slow processes as it begins. After couple of months of focused & due diligent efforts one starts seeing the results emerging.

For example, PMO team is maintaining a wonderful rhythm of interactive discussions and support on schedule development & tracking aspects with a program manager. It is happening for almost 4 to 5 weeks. One fine day, a call comes from the program manager asking the time availability of the PMO member for guidance on some important aspects of schedule tracking. This is indeed a moment of ecstasy.

It can be compared with a moment for a boy when his girl accepts the relationship! One must celebrate. However remember this is not the end. Don't force the things. The relationship has just started evolving. Let it evolve, be patient. Capture on such moments. Offer some new services as gifts. Appreciate that program manager. The PMO team should make a note of this and can mention few such things during all hands presentations where more number of people are present.

It is indeed a fun. These are few basic and extremely important steps must be taken when a contributory PMO is being set up.

Now that we have listed and elaborated these steps, I would like to share the experience of Mr Arvind from Honeywell ITSS division.

I have performed the role of external mentor in last 15 years in many such assignments of setting the contributory PMO. As Arvind says, a combination of Internal Owner with External mentor has always helped. There are couple of incidences where the setting up the contributory PMO was not so effective and I had to accept it. The main reason was the absence of internal owner from the organization. As Arvind mentioned the internal owner is a navigator for the ship. The currents and obstacles in the waters of the organization are known to the internal owner. It reduces the time and energy of the external mentor to discover those. Collaborative approach of internal owner and external mentor always lead to success in setting up the contributory PMO.

Before moving to the next chapter, let's take a small quiz.

Mark the Statements True or False

1. The very first step is to start spreading the word about setting up the PMO. It is advisable to conduct the training sessions on the topic PMO.

2. The essential part of this initial session is to create interest, eagerness and curiosity through entertainment.

3. The initial phase of setting up the PMO is skeptical. People don't tend to trust the PMO members. Once the skepticism phase is crossed, the rest is smooth.

4. PMO set up is more of a psychological forte. It is a mind-set transformational activity.

5. 19 years ago, when it was the first time the author was setting up the PMO internally for Natwest Bank, in Athens, Greece; he received a good support from the project & program managers.

6. Maintaining the team's moral, interactive discussions with project and program managers, assistance on schedule development activities, reviews of the projects and programs, are the examples of one time activities or lesser frequency activities of PMO.

7. It is better to avoid an external mentor while setting up the PMO.

Select the One Right Option from a, b, c, d

8. Most common names suggested for the PMO Set Up project are…

   a. "Schedule Management Service Set Up".

   b. "Program Management Office Set up".

    c. "Setting up PMO".

    d. PMO the backbone of the business success".

9. The author prefers going for more number of smaller projects than lesser number of larger projects while starting the 'Schedule Management Services" The main reason behind this is that...

    a. It reduces the efforts of the PMO team.

    b. It helps spreading the word actively to more number of teams.

    c. This can be started even if the PMO members are not competent.

    d. Schedule is the only important aspect of a project or a program.

10. Contributory PMO members are the change agents. We can also call them as transformation agent. They transform the entire organization to more predictable and adoptive conditions. Select the key behaviour competencies necessary for this from the following.

    i. A person should be able to project reality,

    ii. A person should have courage to speak truth,

    iii. A person should be process oriented,

    iv. A person should have service orientation.

    a. I, II

    b. I, III

    c. II, IV

    d. All of the above.

11. Why do the project & program managers resist PMO?

    a. They are fed up of non-contributory and frequent audits.

    b. They do not get the help, and only need to face audits.

    c. The perceive it as an overhead.

    d. All the above.

12. Which of the following is not an expected result of a Contributory PMO.

    a. Quantitative visibility & predictability is maintained in the aura.

    b. Projects & program selection and prioritization always happens in line with vision, mission.

    c. Consistent & quantitative project performance measurement is missing.

    d. Perceptibly strong support is provided to the project/program mangers by the portfolio managers & strategic sponsors.

For premium exclusive videos, visit https://vimeo.com/ondemand/pmowonderland or contact us at dg@dgonline.in for special discounted prices, quizzes, & 12 PDUs.

Chapter 14

Conclusion

I am sure that you have enjoyed the tour of Wonderland of PMO!. It is thrilling! It was beautiful! It is all about serving wonderfully for the noble and global cause. Isn't it? We were learning the concepts and implementation aspects of project and program management office set up. Of late, PMO is becoming a watchword in the industry. It is indeed a good sign. However one needs to follow certain discipline to seek the maximum yield. This learning intervention "PMO – What Works & What Doesn't?" took you along to practically appreciate the contribution of PMO. This learning intervention. I tried to throw some light on hurdles involved in setting up and sustainably running the PMO in successful manner.

1. We saw the Contributory PMO as a Wonder.
2. We played with **63 strings** of project & program management.
3. We derived the fundamental connection between project & program management with PMO.
4. We saw one real life example of a senior leader demanding the PMO set-up for the name-sake.
5. We then listed **12 characteristics** of the name-sake PMO.
6. We also elaborated on the **4 baskets** of the PMO support.
7. We also enlisted and elaborated **11 functions** of PMO.
8. We elaborated the most important role of the PMO – Competency Development!

9. We took the deep-dive and listed **50 parameters** of the PM Competency Assessment & Development.

10. We elaborated the organizational position & issues involved while setting the PMO.

11. We have also enlisted and elaborated **12 characteristics** of the Contributory PMO.

12. We became aware about **9 issues** that one needs to tackle while setting up a PMO

13. We worked on **8 actions and tips** for setting up the contributory PMO.

The dream is to develop the mind-set of – the organization without PMO.

We sincerely thank you for being there with us through this learning intervention. I hope that it was useful.

References for Answers

Module 2

1. F
2. T
3. T
4. F
5. F
6. F
7. d

Module 3

1. T
2. T
3. T
4. T
5. T
6. F
7. T
8. F
9. F
10. F
11. F
12. d
13. d
14. d

Module 4

1. T
2. T
3. F
4. d
5. d
6. a
7. d
8. a
9. b
10. c
11. a
12. b
13. c
14. d
15. c
16. d
17. b
18. a

Module 5

1. F
2. T
3. T
4. T
5. F
6. F
7. T
8. T
9. T
10. F
11. T

Module 6

1. T
2. T
3. T
4. T
5. d
6. a
7. b
8. a
9. b
10. c
11. a
12. b
13. c
14. d

Module 7

1. T
2. T
3. T
4. T
5. F
6. T
7. F
8. a
9. b
10. c
11. d
12. a
13. c
14. b
15. d
16. d

Module 8

1. T
2. F
3. T
4. T
5. T
6. T
7. F
8. F
9. T

10. T	14. d	18. a
11. a	15. d	19. b
12. a	16. c	
13. c	17. c	

Module 9

1. T	6. T	11. d
2. F	7. a	12. b
3. T	8. b	13. d
4. F	9. b	14. a
5. F	10. c	15. c

Module 10

Module 11

1. F	5. T	9. F
2. F	6. F	10. T
3. T	7. T	11. T
4. T	8. F	

Module 12

1. F	5. F	9. F
2. T	6. T	10. F
3. F	7. T	11. F
4. F	8. F	

Module 13

1. F
2. T
3. F
4. T
5. F
6. T
7. F
8. a
9. b
10. d
11. d
12. c

DGtal Products

Without change there is no innovation, creativity, or incentive for improvement. DG has been always on forefront in this regards. With change in process from PMI, we have introduced some innovative changes in our **DGtal products** as well. We shall be able to satisfy the complete **Talent triangle requirement** of PMI through our Edutainment products.

This is set of Videos which are assets of extremely high value through low cost. With the aspiration to create digital media which can be uses fun and learn technique to impart very important lessons from real life project management and many more changeling and interesting experiences with solutions. PMI too appreciated it a lot and have given clear codes with PDUs. Lots of people then have benefited through this.

References for Answers

Sr	Digital Media	PDUs	Bifurcation for Talent Traingle		
			Technical	Leadership	Strategic
1	Atharvasheersh: A Dialog with self on Project Leadership - The power of subconcious mind!	2	0.5	1.25	0.25
2	PMO: A wonderland - What works & what doesn't? [A complete step by step approach to set up the Project & Program Mgmt office]	12	3	4	5
3	The Jewels of Project Managemet and Leadership Wisdom	2	0.5	1.25	0.25
4	Thirteen Gems - Project Management, Leadership and Strategic Interactions	26	10	8	8
5	Learning PM through Stand-Up Comedy – Project Circus	3	1.5	1	0.5
6	Learning Project Management through Drama - 2016	5	4	1	0
7	Learning Project Management through Drama - 2017	5	4	1	0
8	Animated Revision of PMBOK through Mindmap	1	0.5	0.25	0.25
	Total	56	24	17.75	14.25

Note: Income generated through this products is totally dedicated to educational support to needy in the society.

Our Training & Consulting Services

We provide **Certification Oriented training programs** like and many more www.dgonline.in/pm-courses.php

- PMP® Examination Study Facilitation Workshop.
- PgMP® Examination Study Facilitation Workshop.
- PMI-ACP® Examination Study Facilitation Workshop.
- SAFe: Scaled Agile Framework Certification Workshop.
- PMI-RMP® Examination Study Facilitation Workshop.

We also provide **interactive learning interventions** on topics as listed below and many more. These interventions range from 1 to 4 days. www.dgonline.in/pm-courses.php

- Effective use of Microsoft project.
- Managing Risks effectively.
- PM – a fun filled and interesting endeavour.
- Managing stakeholders.
- Project communications for collaboration.
- Managing anxiety through communication.
- Just enough project & program management.
- Conducting effective reviews of projects & programs.
- Earned value management: how much, for what, by when?

We also provide **services and consulting with personal coaching** on www.dgonline.in/pm-services.php

- Microsoft Project Scheduling Handholding.

- Project & Program Management Office (PMO) Set-up.

- Developing in-house trainers.

- Project Management Competency Assessment.

- MBTI® Based Personal Counselling.

Made in the USA
Middletown, DE
25 May 2020